MARK WHEAWILL

HOW TO MARKET AND SELL YOUR MUSIC AND SURVIVE THE MUSIC BUSINESS IN THE 21st CENTURY

A Comprehensive Guide for all Musicians, Managers and Complete Beginners

HOW TO MARKET AND SELL YOUR MUSIC AND SURVIVE THE MUSIC BUSINESS IN THE 21st CENTURY

A Comprehensive Guide

for all Musicians, Managers and Complete Beginners

MARK WHEAWILL

UPLIFTED PUBLISHING

UPLIFTED PUBLISHING

Manchester. United Kingdom

Tel: +44 (0)161 264 9348

www.upliftedmusic.co.uk

www.upliftedmarketing.co.uk

First published in Great Britain in 2019 by Uplifted Publishing

Printed and bound by Minuteman Press, 120 Manchester Road, Altrincham, Cheshire. WA14 4PY. United Kingdom.

Tel: +44 (0)161 928 8826

www.altrincham.minutemanpress.com

Printed in the UK

CONTENTS

This book is dedicated to the memory of my grandparents who all died when I was young. They never got to see me grow up and I never really got to know them as well as I would have liked to. I hope they are watching over me in heaven and are very proud of their grandchild's achievements in life. We will meet again.

It is also dedicated to my mother and father for all they've done for me throughout my life. I am forever grateful to you both. I love you with all my heart.

This book is also for Zack Marcus David.

And this book is for my future wife and children, if I'm ever lucky enough to be a husband and father. Time will tell!

This book is also for the thousands/millions of genuine musicians on Planet Earth. We are a brotherhood.

"Most of the people focus on success and don't really want to look at failure. Reality is – the more you know how to fail, the more success you'll have! Failing is inevitable and is a lesson. How you come back from failure will define you!"

Dr. Wladimir Klitschk

July 201

ACKNOWLEDGEMENTS

No one helped me with writing this book. I wrote it entirely by myself. However, I'd like to take this opportunity to thank and acknowledge everyone who has played an important role in my life over the years and that has contributed and supported me during my career in the electronic dance music scene. Also, my family for always being there and supporting me throughout my life. Especially with my determination to live my dreams and for always being there through all the ups and downs. It's been one hell of a rollercoaster ride.

Thanks to my mum and dad for your love, support and understanding throughout the years and for encouraging me to do what I really love doing. Thanks for buying me my first guitar and all the other equipment that you bought me when I was in my teenage years and for taking me to band rehearsals. If it wasn't for your love, support and kindness, I would never have been able to do what I do now. Thanks for encouraging me to take up an instrument and do recorder lessons in Junior (Primary) school all those years ago. Even though I hated those lessons, it was my first step on the musical journey. It's what every child needs – supportive parents. I love you very much.

Thanks to my brother David, for letting me take over the bedroom at home when we were youngsters and introducing me to the world of computers. Recording music has never been the same since I dumped my four track multi-track recording device and made the switch over to Cubase VST using Midi Sequencing and Audio Recording software. It made a massive difference to my music productions. It opened up a lot of doors and made all things possible. Thanks to my sister, Lisa, for your love, support and encouragement too.

Thanks to my Uncle Steven and Aunty Linda for all your love and for encouraging me to take up an interest in football and for helping me since I was born. Also, for giving me the opportunities to watch Manchester United Football Club and learn how to run a successful team. It has been very educational!

I'd like to thank Chris Steriopulos for giving me my first break when I was first starting out and making electronic dance music. It was his belief in me, the music and his vision for the future which started this journey back in those days when I was studying for my degree at University. If it wasn't for us meeting at University and his support, who knows, I may never have got my lucky break. He helped provide me with a platform to release my music and gain exposure through his record label – Source Of Gravity Records.

Thanks to Dave Luke (The Jedi Master) for mentoring me and showing me how Cubase worked back in the early days when I did a work placement at your recording studio. It was very helpful and inspirational. I'm surprised we never worked together on any music and did a collaboration. It would have been amazing. There's still time yet!

I'd also like to thank Roydan Styles for your lifelong friendship, support and encouragement. You are a very talented and gifted musician. I hope to see your music on vinyl someday and for you to receive the recognition you deserve. We shall always remain friends. We make a great team too. I hope this is the start of a new era and Uplifted is a great success for us all.

Thanks to Peter Jackson for your friendship over the last 20 years and your support and encouragement. You've stuck by me through thick and thin! It was a pleasure to work with you on our track "Santiago". I hope we soon create a follow up to it and produce another trance anthem. You are a valued friend. Thanks for also providing me with work in the past when I truly needed it pal.

Thanks to Tom Howard. We only just recently met, but I feel it was divine intervention. We share a lot of similar beliefs and you've been a good friend to me just at the time when I really needed it. You are part of the brotherhood of musicians. Thanks for the information about the Sex Pistols which formed some of my research when writing this book. Hopefully, we get to work on some music projects together and you realize your dreams too. Thanks to everyone who has helped in some way or another. You know who you are!

Lastly, I'd like to thank the Lineal Heavyweight Boxing Champion of the world – Tyson Fury. I've never met him in person, but he has been a massive inspiration to me over the last few years. He has demonstrated that anyone can bounce back from illness and mental health issues and be very successful. I've been watching his progress with his career over the years very closely and he has proved that it can be done. He has given me great confidence and self-belief in my own abilities and I would like to acknowledge him for that. Thank you Tyson. I wish you all the best with your career!

FOREWORD

In case you don't know me or if you have never heard of me before, I am an Artist, Record Producer and DJ. I have a B.A. Joint Honour's Degree in Media Studies with Business Management and Information Technology which was an intensive three year course awarded by the University of Manchester in 1999. I also have a Distinction in GNVQ Advanced Level Business which was a two year course and I achieved a B Grade in GCSE Music in High School as well as gaining GCSE's in 9 other subjects. I was also a Company Director of TSYT RECORDINGS Ltd in 2004 – 2006 which was my first record label that I established in the early noughties and its subsidiaries and my dissertation at University was on how to set up and establish a record label.

I had over 35 official single releases on 12" vinyl format on a number of record labels and appeared on several CD compilations around the world between the years 1999 – 2005. I can sing, play the guitar and keyboards and furthermore, I am a songwriter. All in all, I wrote hundreds of tracks when I was growing up. I was also a Synth Programmer and created Third Party Sound Libraries for various hardware and software synthesizers around the same time.

These days, I specialize in Marketing businesses and I have read numerous books on different types of Marketing methods over the years and I currently work in Marketing for my own business – Uplifted Marketing, as a Marketing Executive and Consultant. Please visit my website – www.upliftedmarketing.co.uk for further information.

I'd been thinking of writing a book for a number of years. I'd mentioned the idea a few times to people close to me and on social media. I'd previously written a 12,000 word dissertation back in 1999 as part of my degree course at University College Warrington. I knew how time consuming it would be and the amount of planning that is involved. So, it was always going to be a big undertaking. Plus, I wasn't sure what to write about at first and how it would benefit the reader. Initially, I thought of writing an autobiography but I didn't feel that I had enough to write about just yet at this stage of my life.

But after many months of thinking and making notes on different subject matters, I finally decided to put pen to paper and make it a reality. I knew I was capable of writing a book and had the self-belief and initiative to do it. It was just a case of putting words into action. It was going to be part biography and part music industry advice. I thought I'd combine the music marketing side of the music business with a lot of my own experiences throughout my youth and my early career as an electronic dance music producer and DJ in the dance music industry.

The idea behind the book is to help people and to share valuable information and knowledge which will benefit the reader considerably. The objective is to inspire people – mainly other musicians, artists and bands and provide tips, advice and insights into the music business. This book isn't just for novices and beginners, it's also for people who have been involved in music for a long time or for those that are just simply curious. It is also a way of getting my message across and educating people about the constant struggle that many of us face in the music industry nowadays.

This book is like an extension of my dissertation which I wrote all those years ago and provides a thorough guide on how to market your music and establish a major record company in the 21st century and how to overcome all the challenges we currently face in 2018 and beyond. I have years of wisdom on my side now and I know all the pros and cons of the business and how to increase the chances of being much more successful and not making the same mistakes again.

I understand the impact that the worldwide web has had on the music industry since its inception more than most. I was an internet geek back in the early days in the nineties before the internet became very popular and in the days before social media. I used to use the internet a lot and would make friends with people from all over the globe and chat to them in Yahoo Chat Rooms and on ICQ and on Yahoo Messenger and I would share my music with them in the days before I first signed my first record deals with other labels. I even used Napster at one point. Additionally, I predicted the future of the music industry with regards to downloading and file sharing and also streaming which people were calling pay-per-play at the time.

I consider myself as an expert when it comes to computers and the internet. Information Technology is my forte. I know it inside and out. I understand the technology and know it better than most people. I am not fooled by technical jargon either like others are. I am also a pioneer and I like to lead by example and show my fellow community of musicians, artists and bands the way forward in the 21st century and improve their lives and how to create prosperity within their own communities. After all, we are a brotherhood and a special breed so we need to look out for each other. I spent years living on baked beans and getting by on the breadline and suffering from major depression. None of us have to struggle or put up with modern forms of slavery and exploitation anymore!

Music is a talent which we all share and it is a valuable commodity. We don't always get the respect we deserve for our talents and all the time we sacrifice and the effort we put into learning music theory and practicing instruments, especially at a young age. If it weren't for us musicians, there wouldn't be a music industry. It's that simple! We have the power. We just need to take the power back!

Whether you're a novice, a manager representing artists and bands or looking to set up your own record company, this book will provide you with a very useful guide and teach you what to do, what not to do and how to overcome any obstacles that may block your path in the music business. Throughout this book, I show you ways in which to do this and achieve those goals and objectives. I'd like to take this opportunity to thank you for buying my book and taking the time to read it. I can assure you, it is worth every penny! I hope you thoroughly enjoy reading it and that my book helps you on your journey and it benefits you greatly.

Mark Wheawill - July 2018

HOW IT ALL BEGAN!

When I was a child, like most other children, I heard music on the radio and on TV. We only had a few radio stations on the old vintage transistor radio (FM/AM) in our home and a few TV channels in them days – BBC 1, BBC 2 and ITV as far as I can remember. That was my only exposure to music in them days as we didn't have the likes of the internet and MTV. So, if you were born before then or around the same time you'll know that most children grew up listening to music which their parents liked and played. The same still applies to this day for children growing up, only there is a lot more access to music what with the development of the worldwide web and mobile phones.

I was the first of three children born to my parents – my mother and father. I was given the name Mark Wheawill (pronounced "way-will") on my birth certificate. I was born on October 20th in 1976 at the local hospital which was called "Park Hospital" at the time where the NHS (National Health Service) first began in Manchester, UK. I was the eldest child in my family (I have a younger brother and sister) and was quite a shy child really! It took me a very long time to get over my shyness, that I can tell you.

Me and my brother, David (who is 2 years and 2 months younger than me), lived in a semi-detached house in a small village called Flixton in Manchester for most of our childhood. I started going through my mum and dad's record collection which was on tape and vinyl in those days when I was in junior school (primary school which it is called nowadays). So, at a guess, I must have been aged around 6, 7 or 8, although I did take a lot of music in subconsciously before then that was played on the radio and on TV etc. After that, it became somewhat of an obsession. I'd read through all the inlays of the records whilst listening to all of my mum and dad's music collection. Well not quite all of it, but most! Artists and bands that particularly stood out for me in their music collection were: Abba, Jackson Five, Michael Jackson, Pink Floyd, Santana, Curiosity Killed The Cat, Level 42, Gypsy Kings, Mike Oldfield, Dire Straits, lots of Motown and soul artists and many more!

I'd often sing along to Michael Jackson's "Thriller" album and try and emulate his singing voice and record my vocals on to a retro reel-to-reel recording device which my Aunty Joyce gave me. My dad would often burst into my bedroom asking if I'd done my homework for school! It would infuriate me at the time. I got the impression my father wasn't too keen on me singing. Looking back, it probably didn't seem macho and manly enough. He was very strict in them days and put me under a lot of pressure to perform well at school and achieve the desired results to keep him happy and content. I did eventually live up to those expectations and gained good results in school. However, little did my parents know, I had other plans. I knew from a very early age what I wanted to do with my life.

My first ever purchase on vinyl record was Debbie Gibson's "Shake your love" which was a 7" vinyl single released in the 1980's. It was a huge single for her and a hit record at the time. Not long after, I bought Def Leppard's "Hysteria" album on 12" vinyl too from the local Woolworths store in Urmston or Stretford (I can't recall which particular store it was exactly!) as that was the main place to go to buy music in those days. I loved going through all the tapes and vinyl records at the store. It was very exciting and all new to me. Those were my first memories of my love affair with music and they were very fond memories indeed.

My mum and dad sent me for recorder lessons when I was at Wellacre Junior School in Flixton. I was about 8 years old. It was a woodwind instrument and in all honesty, I used to hate going to the lessons. I had no interest in learning the instrument whatsoever. It just didn't seem very cool. At the time, I preferred going outside at break times and playing football on the school playground with all my friends and I started taking an interest in the opposite sex. The only music I ever really learnt to play on the recorder was "Three blind mice", which I can still play to this day as it was so easy to remember and perform on the instrument. I'm not sure what happened to the instrument though.

It wasn't until I was sent to Lymm High school in Cheshire which was out of the catchment area, that I started to take an interest in musical instruments and learn to play the guitar when I was aged about 13. My dad had a cheap acoustic guitar which he had bought out of a Kay's catalogue and I used to borrow it and practice playing regularly. It hurt my fingers like hell at the beginning as most guitarists know until you develop pads on your fingers. In fact, the first time I tried playing the guitar, I quit as I was not getting anywhere. It was extremely frustrating. I wasn't making much progress. But something inside me decided to have another go and this time I found it a lot easier to play at the second attempt. I guess that's been the story of my life. Perseverance seems to pay off! I'm not a quitter. I would offer to do the washing up in the kitchen if my parents would buy me a guitar of my own. Eventually, they did by me one. It was an electric guitar. Something similar to a Fender Stratocaster, but a cheaper version. Anyway, I was self-taught and learnt to play the guitar myself and was making good progress. It was the same with the singing.

I carried on singing and learning to play the guitar and eventually formed and joined a heavy metal band with a drummer from Frodsham in Cheshire, who was in my form at school called Peter Gray (he got bullied a lot by a few other kids in school). We performed on stage at the Christmas concert in High School in front of all the other school children. Our art teacher, Mr. Moulding played lead guitar on stage with us. I was a rhythm guitarist at the time and a guy called Andrew Ranson was on the vocals. We played cover versions of Guns N' Roses tracks "Sweet Child O' Mine" and "Knockin' On Heaven's Door". I played the lead guitar solo on "Sweet Child O' Mine"! I can't begin to tell you how nervous I felt. That was my introduction to the entertainment business and my first performance on stage in front of hundreds of people. I was aged just 13!

I was also a keen footballer in my early days and had previously played for the local football team called Flixton Junior's under the management, mentoring and coaching of a really nice guy called Ron Massey, who unfortunately died a few years later after I'd joined. I started off as a defender and was also the vice-captain for my junior school football team. I scored a few goals playing for both my school team and the local junior team and captained the side in a 5 or 6 aside competition. I also got bullied a lot by some of the other players on the team at Flixton Junior's. That put me off playing in a team for quite a while and made me very weary of people growing up. I did eventually toughen up, but then people became very weary of me as I took no abuse from anyone after that and people knew not to mess with me.

I later went on to play for a local semi-professional club called "Trafford FC" in my late teenage years for a brief period but things didn't quite work out and I lost my confidence as a player. Also, not long after leaving and joining another local amateur football team called "Woodsend FC", I broke my ankle in training as soon as we kicked off. I had to be carried off and helped to hospital to get a plaster cast put on. So, I think that put me off playing football in a big way. I did go on to play for another local amateur team called "Aldermere FC" and scored a hat-trick in one particular game when I played on the right-wing. I scored two goals from near to the half-way line and chipped the goalkeeper perfectly. The first time I couldn't believe it myself but then I tried it again from more or less the same spot. It was no fluke. It even amazed me. I had the same kind of precision that David Beckham had when he played at Manchester United Football Club. I used to practice free kicks a lot on the field near to where I lived at the time, so I guess the hard work paid off! I remember doing the same thing in another game for Aldermere FC too. I would also sometimes play up front as a striker or centre-forward. Scoring goals was what I enjoyed the most. However, I wasn't much of a team player in those days.

My Uncle Steven used to take me to a few football games at Old Trafford to see Manchester United Football Club play. At the time, they were managed by Ron Atkinson when I first went to watch them. This was before the glory days under Sir Alex Ferguson who I met once at the Soccer Six tournament at the G-MEX Arena in Manchester City Centre and I managed to get his autograph. Little did I know how successful Manchester United Football Club would become under the leadership of Sir Alex. Sir Alex Ferguson was a great role model and a massive inspiration for me when I look back at those early days of my life.

So, during my childhood, all that seemed to matter to me was girls, football and music. I didn't really take much interest in anything else. I eventually went on to form another band called "Caricatura" (which later became known as "Caricature") with fellow students - Peter Gray, the drummer, Justin Haigh on lead guitar and Paul Cunningham, the bassist and Andrew Fish on keyboards. The band took on many different lineups over the course of time, but eventually we settled with those musicians I've named above. We performed many gigs at the local village hall in a place called High Legh in Cheshire and at Lymm High School and at other venues in front of hundreds of people and wrote a lot of our own music. One of the highlights was our gig at Jilly's Rockworld in Manchester in about 1993.

We were also invited to record at Jerusalem recording studio in Manchester City Centre after winning a competition they were hosting. The last band at high school I was in was called "Pop Love Haze" which was heavily influenced by the grunge music scene. We were all into bands such as Pearl Jam, Brad, Satchel, Soundgarden, Temple Of The Dog, Alice In Chains, Stone Temple Pilots, Smashing Pumpkins, Nirvana, Mudhoney, Sonic Youth, Metallica, Rage Against The Machine and indie bands like Radiohead etc. Pop Love Haze consisted of myself on vocals and rhythm guitar, Justin Haigh on lead guitar and backing vocals, Paul Cunningham on bass guitar and Greg Haigh (Justin's younger brother) on the drums. We became a very popular band at school.

We wrote lots of our own material and eventually released an album on tape cassette which we put together and had recorded on my Yamaha 4-track multi-tracker and sold it to fellow school students. The artwork on the front cover of the album which I originally designed caused somewhat of a stir amongst the female students at school and I remember Justin Haigh having to re-design the front cover for it, as not to offend anyone! Some of our most popular songs which we wrote were called "I ain't wrong", "These eyes" and "Destiny". These were big favourite's amongst our student following. Collectively, we inspired a lot of children too back then. We were child stars and exceptionally talented for our age.

I also learnt to play the piano and keyboards when I was aged 16. My dad had a good synthesizer collection in his bedroom at our home. His dad played piano as a session musician once for The Searchers. I used to play on his keyboards and make my own sounds. At one particular gig which we performed at as Pop Love Haze at Lymm High School in front of our parents and other school children, my grandma came along to watch the concert. My mum informed me that my grandma commented "I never knew Mark could play the piano!". Neither did many other people, it came as a big surprise to most but demonstrated that I was multi-talented and naturally gifted at music.

I also met a local guy called Roydan Styles (who has since gone on to become a lifelong friend) during a time when I was out delivering the local Messenger newspaper near to where I lived at the time in Flixton. He is a very gifted musician and is a very talented singer/songwriter and guitarist. Someone who I respect very much and have a lot of time for. His vocals in the early days reminded me of John Lennon from the Beatles. Roydan was heavily influenced by Roy Harper as well as the Beatles. Roydan has even supported Nick Harper and Roy Harper (who appeared on Pink Floyd's "Wish You Were Here" album) at gigs throughout the years.

We became acquainted just outside his parent's home on Derwent Road in Flixton on that fateful day when I was delivering the local newspaper for a pittance. He had his Walkman (which is the equivalent of an I-POD in the 21st century) with him at the time and played me some of his own music on tape. I was very impressed with the production and the way it sounded and it inspired me in many ways. We did a few gigs together and recorded a few tracks as part of a collaboration on our multi-track recording devices.

This is how I started getting into the production and sound engineering side of music. I was also influenced by Record Producer's such as Brendan O'Brien (Stone Temple Pilots/Black Crowes) and John Mutt Lange (Shania Twain/Def Leppard). I later went on to be inspired by other producer's such as B.T. Roydan is part of the team here at Uplifted Music these days. I originally founded the new label in 2010 and it is my second record label. I will tell you more about the new record label later on in this chapter and other chapters. My first record label was called TSYT Recordings which I officially started in about 2002.

4

I went to a lot of gigs in my teens and early twenties. The first ever concert I went to was at the Manchester Apollo to see Ozzy Osbourne in about 1992. The second concert I went to see was Metallica at the G-MEX in Manchester, also in 1992 with my dad. I did a lot of "head banging" to the music that evening and suffered from whiplash the next day. So, I never head banged ever again! I'm surprised I didn't suffer from brain damage. Over the years, I've seen many other bands perform live such as Depeche Mode (at least 3 times!), Pearl Jam, Christina Aguilera, Kylie, Brad, The Prodigy, The Chemical Brothers, Orbital, Jamiroquai, Spiritualized, Radiohead, Faithless, Soundgarden, Moby, Mansun, Stone Temple Pilots, The Corrs, Goldfrapp, Starsailor, Corinne Bailey-Rae, Mark Ronson, Unklejam, Ozric Tentacles, Roy Harper, Wizards Of Twiddly and Nick Harper and many more acts.

I've also seen countless DJ's performing at clubs such as at the legendary Sankey's in Manchester City Centre and Cream at Nation in Liverpool. Sankey's is closed down now but I have fond memories of those nights in the early noughties. I saw Sasha, John Digweed, Lee Burridge, Masters At Work, The Stanton Warriors, Tilt, Quivver, Evolution, James Holden, Keith McDonnell and numerous other DJ's. My memory is very hazy though for obvious reasons if you were a clubber in them days! I'll leave it to your imagination as to the reason why.

A lot of the DJ's I've mentioned in this last paragraph, I've also met in the past when I used to go out socializing in the electronic dance music scene. I never went to the Hacienda as I was a latecomer to the world of dance music. Too be honest with you, I believe the Hacienda was overhyped! I walked past it once on a night out in the city centre of Manchester and I peered through a gap in the door and it looked like a dirty warehouse with a dance floor on it. It didn't look anything special to me. I personally didn't see the attraction and know what all the fuss was about. Sankey's was my favourite club in Manchester. I would have loved to have DJ'd there!

The last ever band I played in was called "Splitscreen". This was Peter Gray's new band at the time. Peter's older brother went to the same school as Gary Barlow from Take That. Dave Hatchard and Ben Goldsmith (who were also from the Frodsham area in Cheshire) were on the guitars and Keith Baker was the bass guitarist. I was standing in for their female vocalist and we played a few gigs at the Night & Day Café and at the Boardwalk in Manchester in 1999. As per usual though, I was very shy and suffered from stage fright! I haven't ever played in a band since then and that was the last time I was ever in a rock band performing on stage. However, I hope to change this in the future and put together a new band and perform live at gigs playing new material. If I do, it will be a fusion of electronic dance music, rock and many other genres.

The next major development in my music career came when I went to University College Warrington in 1996. I was studying for a Media and Business Management and I.T. (Information Technology) Joint Honour's Degree at the campus and met a Progressive House music DJ from the Isle Of Man, by the name of Christian Steriopulos on the Business module which was part of the course I was attending at the time. We quickly became good friends and he invited me to his room on campus and played me a lot of Progressive House/Trance music including such acts as BT (Brian Transeau) who is an American Electronic Dance Music Producer and a pioneer of Progressive House/Trance music and DJ mixes by the legendary British DJ's Sasha and Digweed.

Christian Steriopulos (A.K.A Chris Sterio) introduced me to BT's first album - "IMA" which was a massive inspiration at the time. I had never heard music quite like it! I was already writing and producing Trance and Drum N' Bass music and sending my demo's to magazines such as Future Music, Muzik and Sound On Sound for reviews. One of my tracks under my "Marcus W" alias called "Simultaneous" featured on the cover CD of Future Music magazine in the UK – Issue 83, June 1999.

Not long after I started university, I bought a couple of synthesizer's from Dawson's Music Shop in Warrington – a Korg Trinity and a Korg Prophecy (which both Depeche Mode and The Prodigy used on some of their albums) out of the money I got from my student loan. It was a wise investment. I was not living on campus at University at the time and was commuting by train to Warrington from Manchester and sometimes I'd also cycle the 14 miles there and back, so, I didn't have to pay any rent and I could afford to buy the synths and start using them on new tracks I was writing. It proved to be one of the best investments I ever made and one of the wisest choices I'd ever make.

All of my band mates from the Pop Love Haze days had gone their separate ways and it was only me left continuing the music dream. So, making electronic dance music as a solo artist seemed like the next logical progression. Things were starting to fall into place and I was getting more and more confident and had the self-belief that I could make it in the music industry. I was sad in a way that my former band mates never continued with the band we'd put together, especially after all the hard work and effort we'd put into it all over the years and the following which we had. But, who was I to tell them what to do with their lives?

I'd also sent demos of my music to record label's such as Positiva, Freeform Records, Talkin Loud Records and Good Looking Records which was owned by LTJ Bukem. In most instances, I received very good reviews and feedback. I was well on course to becoming a successful electronic dance music producer. I just needed to step up my production by purchasing more quality studio equipment and then the dream would be realized and come true! That's how I looked at it at the time. The money side of the business never once crossed my mind. I was so passionate and enthusiastic about music and I had the abilities to make my dreams come true, the money side never crossed my mind once. I was determined to stick at it, no matter what. I never really thought about the business side of things when it came to music production. Later on in my life, I would learn to regret it and wish I'd had a manager to take care of me and guide me in the right direction.

The big break came when Chris Steriopulos, my friend from University, decided to start his own Progressive House/Trance music record label back in 1999 called "Source Of Gravity Records" and he pressed up a 12" white label vinyl record of one of my tracks and handed it to various club DJ's. At around the same time, I had launched a business of my own called "Onlinesoundproduction.com" which I was running from my bedroom at my parents' home whilst I was at university. It did very well and helped pay for a lot of the equipment which I purchased.

Chris eventually signed a Pressing and Distribution deal with Unique Distribution which was based in Bolton whilst I was away for two months travelling around West Virginia in America in 2000 in search of love. He never thought of consulting me though at the time and to this day, I do not know what kind of deal he signed with them but later on in life, I got the impression that I had been scammed as I never received any royalties from any of the releases on Source Of Gravity Records and Gravitation Records. But yet, they were quite happy to keep releasing my music which seemed very strange to me and didn't make much business sense at all. Unique Distribution eventually went out of business later on in life.

I was making Third Party Sound Libraries for the Korg Trinity synthesizer and selling them via mail order and I used any income it generated to pay for some of the synths I bought further down the line and to build up my own home recording studio. Whilst balancing my studies and running my own business, I was also working at Asda as a store assistant on the garden centre outside and also in the home and leisure department which was just opposite the Trafford Shopping Centre on Trafford Park in Manchester as it was being built.

Also, around the time I was at University College Warrington, I met a very good friend of mine called Dave Luke ("The Jedi Master" as I always called him!) at his Faze 9 Recording Studio in Flixton. This was during my university work placement which lasted for 9 weeks. As it transpired, he had also had records released on a number of Progressive House/Trance music label's and appeared on one of the very first Gatecrasher album's on CD. He recorded under such names as Loco Parentis with DJ Big Danny (another local DJ) who gigs under his own name – Andy Daniels, these days. Andy has worked for Hed Kandi and supported many big name DJ's during his career and was a resident DJ at 2 Kinky at the View in Frodsham, Cheshire. That's how I got my gig there in 2003 through an introduction to the owner of the club.

Whilst, I was on my work placement at Dave Luke's Faze 9 Recording Studio, I also met a DJ called Jason Herd at his studio who was a client of his at the time. In later years, Jason went on to produce a classic hit single under the name of Herd & Fitz featuring Abigail Bailey on vocals called "I just can't get enough" which reached Number 11 in the UK charts back in 2005. At the time I met him, Dave was helping him produce earlier house tracks which he had released on various record labels. I also used to play that particular track in a lot of my own DJ sets when I was spinning house music.

Later on, Dave Luke formed an electronic music duo with Andy Chester called "My Computer" when they were both living in Urmston in Manchester which received great plaudits. In the past they were signed to Creation Records (the same label Oasis were signed to) or at least Andy was. The new band – My Computer signed a music publishing deal with BMG and was managed at one stage by Derek Ryder of Hot Soup Management (Shaun Ryder's dad! (of the famous Manchester indie band – The Happy Monday's)). My Computer released two official albums in all when they were signed to BMG. Their second album "No CV" was produced by John Leckie (who also produced The Stone Roses and Radiohead to give you some examples and he was the Tape Op for the Beatles) whom I met a couple of times when I went down to their studio sessions in Urmston. I learnt a lot from watching them all in the studio.

As part of the media module of my degree course at university, I was also involved in Commercial Music Production in the recording studio which was based on the campus and I helped produce an album of bands called "DNA" on the university label – Resolution Records in 1999. One of the bands that featured on the album which I helped produce was a local band from Manchester called "Flood" which I highly rated at the time. Somehow though, they never made it big as far as I am aware! They reminded me of Manchester's own version of U2 in many ways. I often wondered what happened to them.

When I was young, I didn't socialize much. I stayed in at home a lot during my early teenage years learning to sing, playing the guitar and keyboards and producing music. I missed out on a social life and socializing in general and didn't have the social skills that most people around my age had learnt as a result of this. So, in many ways it hampered my progress. Most of my high school friends lived miles away, so, I was unable to play out with them and develop my social skills and relationships and I had lost touch with most friends that lived locally. When I look back at my early life, I do believe I had some minor autistic traits. Especially, the shyness and I was not able to communicate as effectively as most other children. I wasn't the most social person either but somehow I managed to make it through school life and on to university.

My first ever official release was Source Of Gravity "Futuristic Visions" in 2000 on Source Of Gravity Records. You cannot begin to imagine how excited I was at this and the expectations which came with it all. My dreams were starting to come true! It's difficult to explain the feeling I had when my music was released on a vinyl record and spinning on the turntable. I was elated. I had countless other records released in the years that followed. Over 35 in all! My most successful records were Vitality "Skylite" which was released on Method Records back in 2003 and which was supported by Superstar DJ's such as Armin Van Buuren on his "A State Of Trance" radio show in Holland, Sasha, Paul Oakenfold and Nick Warren (Way Out West), to name just a few.

The track was also Tune of the Month in IDJ magazine in the UK receiving 5 out of 5 in the Progressive House music reviews section. It also received airplay on Manchester's KEY 103 FM radio station (now called "Hits Radio"). The original mix of "Skylite" also featured on a dance music compilation CD called "Solid Sounds" in Belgium. Among the artists included on that compilation were Queen, Sinead O'Connor, Tomcraft and IIO! I featured amongst some huge names.

Another track which I produced called "Indecisive" with a guy called Gary Morris (A.K.A Didge, who played the didgeridoo) under the name of Evenflow was released on 12" vinyl on Baroque Records in 2002, a record label which is based in Coventry in the UK. This particular track was a massive hit on the underground scene and was also supported by some big name DJ's such as Tilt and Quivver and was played at super clubs like Cream in Liverpool. It sold over a few thousand copies. I recorded under many different pseudonyms between the years 1999 – 2005: Mark Wheawill, Evenflow (with Gary Morris), Source Of Gravity (with Chris and Olly Steriopulos), Vitality, Outlanders (with Chris Steriopulos), TSYT, Bravemusic (with Gary Morris) and 4th Orbit (with Chris Steriopulos, Sean McClellan and Gordon Carpenter) in North Carolina, USA. I even worked on a remix project with Tilt at one point at their studio in Stoke.

Other significant tracks I was involved in were Source Of Gravity "Perseverance" which I sang on and wrote and produced the music for. Chris Steriopulos wrote the lyrics. It received Recommended Tune of the Month in IDJ magazine in 2003 and Mark Wheawill "Transition" which I also wrote and produced and sang on was released on Baroque Records (in 2003) and yet again, it received Recommended Tune of the Month in IDJ magazine. My "Future House Mix" of "Transition" was included on the Coors Light Party-A-Go-Go dance music compilation in Taiwan. It was the only record I ever licensed to a compilation on my first record label – TSYT RECORDINGS in 2004. Adam Freeland and GusGus also featured on the compilation!

I appeared on a cover CD of 7 magazine (UK) called "Baroque In Session 2002" which was mixed by Parks & Wilson and of which was given away as a free promo with the magazine. This particular release featured my tracks – Evenflow "Indecisive" (Original Vocal Mix) which I also sang on and a track called – Bravemusic "Spiritualized" (Mark Wheawill's Eat Your Heart Out Baby Dub) which was originally released on Method Records back in 2002. "Spiritualized" was also Number 1 in the Tune Inn Records hype chart. I featured amongst more big artists such as Maria Nayler and Satoshi Tomiie.

Other notable compilations which my music was featured on was a compilation released in Greece in about 2001 called "Spacer – Europe's future anthems". My track Source Of Gravity "Futuristic Visions" was included on it and we featured amongst many big names in the dance music fraternity such as Paul Oakenfold, ATB and Da Rude. I also featured on several other dance music compilations on CD. Some of which I never even received a copy of from the record label's I was signed to at the time, which I thought was highly unprofessional and disrespectful!

When I first started DJ'ing I played at a lot of house parties in and around the areas of Burnley, Accrington, Todmorden and Nelson. I also played in Leeds and Urmston in Manchester and at a cave party on Mount Rydal in the Lake District in the UK. I played a purely Progressive House set overlooking a lake. That night went down in history and was seen as legendary by all who attended the free party. It was one of the most crazy nights I ever took part in. There were about a hundred people camped outside this cave on the top of the mountain and everyone was off their heads on drugs.

I even helped carry the generators up to the top of the mountain where the cave was situated. It was no easy task let me tell you that. The whole night went on until about 8 am in the morning. A local resident out walking his dog suggested we shut down the event at this time which we did do. I think the music was amplified by the shape of the cave and echoed throughout the whole village that evening and morning. God only knows what they thought of it all?

I was invited to DJ on Manchester's KEY 103 FM in 2003 on a Saturday evening for a 2 hour guest mix to an estimated audience of over 15,000 listeners. I also played a 2 hour DJ set at 2 Kinky at The View in Frodsham, Cheshire to approximately 1000 people. I was warm up for Oliver Lang. They never invited me back because I played all my best records and upset the headlining DJ! However, the clubbers seemed to really enjoy the night as they were all on the dancefloor dancing away by the time I finished my set. The room was packed and it was a thoroughly enjoyable evening. DJ Big Danny (Andy Daniels) told me to play my best records. So, I did exactly that! That was one of my best ever gigs.

That same year I also travelled to Lisbon in Portugal and did 3 gigs in 5 days. I hardly slept, but it was worthwhile. The only thing I didn't enjoy was how lonely I felt. Not many people spoke English and I missed my girlfriend at the time! I also played on a college radio station in Colombia, South Carolina in the USA. That was about as far as I'd get in those days with regards to my DJ'ing career before I became seriously ill. The impression I got was that a lot of other DJ's saw me as major competition and as a threat and as though I was overstepping the boundaries and treading on their territory. After about a year of practicing on the turntables, I was a natural and had developed my own technique for mixing records. I was never made aware of any unwritten codes amongst DJ circles so I just did my own thing and played music that I really liked. It was just a way of getting exposure for the music.

In the meantime, I was running my own Sound Production business and working several jobs. I was a Customer Service Advisor at O2 Telecommunications for just under a year working in Preston Brook, near to Runcorn in Cheshire. I then started working as a Temporary Clerical Assistant at AQA in Rusholme in Manchester for just over three years. Whilst, I was doing all of this, I was working on new music and in the process of starting my own record label – TSYT RECORDINGS.

By about 2004, I had eventually built up a recording studio of my own that I could be majorly proud of which was worth somewhere in the region of £30,000, just to give you an idea of the costs involved in making and producing music. I worked very hard to afford everything over a number of years. My studio consisted of a large number of synthesizers such as the Access Virus Rack, Korg MS2000/R, Korg Trinity, Korg Prophecy, Novation Nova Laptop, Waldorf Micro Q and Waldorf Microwave XT. I was using Cubase VST as my DAW (Digital Audio Workstation) for midi sequencing and recording audio and I was able to afford microphones such as the Neumann TLM 103 and an Avalon Valve Mic Pre Amp which cost £2000, Akai S5000 Sampler, Focusrite Compressors and TC Electronic Fireworx and Lexicon Multi-Effects Processors as well as other music production equipment which weren't cheap, believe me! I owned a studio that most bedroom producers would have envied and been very jealous of.

It was rare that I ever got paid an advance fee from most of the record labels that signed and released my music. Baroque Records and Method Records owned and run by Keith McDonnell (Innate) were the most consistent paying of all them and the most professional looking back. However, I still felt that I was being underpaid and taken advantage of and not as highly valued as I expected to be. I was a rising star in the Progressive House/Trance music scene and I was starting to accumulate a lot of debt due to the outlay on everything. I managed to get Keith to release me from any contractual obligations and commitments to Baroque/Method Records and all the rights of the records that were released on their labels were reverted back to me.

Between 2002-2004, I started to write and produce my first album. It was eventually released on my own record label – TSYT RECORDINGS in 2004. By the year 2004, I decided to leave the labels I was signed to and managed to get back the rights to some of my back catalogue including Vitality "Skylite", Mark Wheawill "Transition" and Evenflow "Indecisive". I self-financed the production, manufacture, marketing and release of my debut album – Vitality "Vitality" on CD and eventually it led to bankruptcy in 2006. I found myself in over £80,000's of debt. I only pressed up 1000 copies.

In the end, it was a major financial disaster! I rarely ever got paid by any of the record label's I was signed to at the start of my dance music career and I didn't receive much in the way of royalties. They always used to come up with the excuse that they couldn't afford to pay an advance to sign my records. This had a major knock on effect. Hence, why I decided to part company with the likes of Baroque Records, Method Records and Source Of Gravity Records in order to start covering all my costs and pay my bills by selling my own music.

Things didn't quite turn out the way I expected them to though. There was no way I was ever going to be able to pay it all back unless some miracle took place. I ended up falling out with a lot of people in the process. I would have been enslaved for the rest of my life and would have had to work even harder than I already had in order to pay off the interest alone on the loans I took out. It was starting to take a toll on my health and it was making me ill!

However, the album did receive some rave reviews in some magazines, both online and in print. One magazine compared me to Moby. It was also stocked in some HMV stores. I also released a single from the album called "Chemistry" on 12" vinyl white label as a promo. It was a rare release and only 500 copies were ever pressed up and in circulation. It included a Club Mix of "Chemistry" and a track called "Blinded by the sun (Ode To BT)" which was a tribute track I wrote to BT which was inspired by the epic American Progressive House/Trance Music Producer – BT (Brian Transeau). The single never quite made it to the stage of official release as things took a turn for the worse by then.

At one stage in either 2003 or 2004, a friend, Gary Morris who I worked with on some previous tracks at his garage studio in Radcliffe, told me that my music career "had been stopped" as though there were some kind of music industry mafia controlling musicians and their careers and their destinies. He told me that just a few people own the dance music business. I don't know whether he was simply the messenger passing on this information or whether he was implying that he personally had put a so called stop to my dance music production career and DJ'ing or whether other people such as tycoons or labels I had been signed to previously had put a block on my career.

I thought it was a very strange thing to say at the time and I found it quite concerning in all honesty. Just writing about all of this brings back painful memories. Most people involved in the dance music scene are control freaks it would seem and they end up turning on you! It's all about the money with these people no matter what they say. So, it left me with little choice but to start releasing my own music and press on regardless. I did start to receive a lot of abuse from people who I thought were friends at the time. They were a very strange bunch. Not the kind of people I would like to associate with ever again.

Gary did offer to buy a farm house at one point too. He said he was going to build a recording studio in it. I didn't really take him seriously and turned down the offer as he was not prepared to employ me or provide me with a contract for work. I saw no point in doing it when I had a studio of my own. Later on, I found it very difficult getting my music back out there and it seemed as though I was being boycotted not just by the scene but by DJ's as well.

Also, in 2005, I started to have mental health problems. The stress of being in so much debt was starting to get to me and took its toll. It was a heavy burden and a massive weight on my shoulders. I was working so hard and doing everything myself. I was completely exhausted and some people were calling me a freak of nature and a machine at the time I was living in Chorlton in Manchester. It was starting to make me paranoid amongst many other incidents that took place which one day I will speak openly about in the future. I'll save it all for another book.

I had also completed a couple of bootleg remixes of Christina Aguilera's "Ain't No Other Man" which you can listen to on YouTube and a lot of people were asking me for copies of the record. I approached Sony BMG to see if they were interested in licensing the remixes but no such luck! By this time, I became really ill and I was nearly sectioned under the mental health act. To this day, I still believe there was a major conspiracy to keep me under control and ensure that I failed at my attempt to become an independent artist releasing music on my own record label. There were a lot of people trying to get me hooked on various drugs at the time too and I was starting to attract a lot of bad energy.

I ended up spending the next ten years or so in the mental health system going around in circles. The medication I was prescribed just dulled all of my senses and I lost all drive and enthusiasm for making music after that. It was hell on earth to be honest with you. Not only, did I lose all my studio equipment through bankruptcy but everything I had worked so hard for had gone in a flash. I ended up living in Stretford in Manchester for about 3 years and then moved back to Flixton for another 4 years living in some bedsit. At the time, the psychiatrist diagnosed me as having a delusional disorder and that I was in a paranoid psychosis. Nowadays, I have come to the conclusion that I was suffering from PTSD (Post Traumatic Stress Disorder) and serious depression. A few years back, I also started to notice that I was going slightly deaf.

I had a hearing test in about 2016 and it was recorded as high frequency hearing loss on my right side. One of the hazards of working in the music industry. However, I learnt that I had mild sensorineural hearing loss in 2018 after another hearing test which confirmed my previous suspicions. I have trouble hearing people talking to me when there is significant background noise. All brought on through working in noisy environments over the last 20 years or so and from listening to music loud on my headphones as a DJ. My father did warn me of the dangers when I was in my teens but I took very little notice of what he said. In another ten years, I may need to start learning sign language if I continue to expose myself to further work in noisy environments. Is it a risk worth taking? Only time will tell!

In about 2010, I launched my second record label in a voluntary capacity – "Uplifted Music" and re-released my Vitality "Vitality" album on the highly controversial streaming service Spotify, along with a charity compilation called the "Uplifted Music: Cancer Research UK Dance Music

Compilation" which featured 16 underground electronic dance music tracks donated by various artists including myself to help raise funds and awareness for Cancer Research UK which is something I felt strongly about at the time.

Unfortunately, as most people have started to realize, Spotify never pay any royalties to artists, unless the music is being streamed millions of times by subscribers using their streaming service, so, I was unable to ever donate any of the proceeds to the charity. This was highly disappointing as you can imagine! The releases never received a single penny. I have since gone on to campaign against the likes of Spotify and I encourage all artists to remove their music repertoire from Spotify and other streaming services as they are corrupt to the core like most record labels appear to be. I will speak about this matter in a later chapter.

In 2017, I started volunteering and DJ'ing again and became a presenter on the local hospital radio station – Radio Wishing Well and had a regular show called "Eclectricity" on Tuesday evenings from 9pm – 12am. The show featured an eclectic mix of music from Rock, Country, Dance, Pop, Soul, Motown, 80's, Disco, Folk, Classical and much more! I supported the likes of rising country music stars such as Kelsea Ballerini (An American country artist who is based in Nashville, Tennessee) who is tipped to be the next Taylor Swift and also Dua Lipa! A lot of the shows were recorded and uploaded to my Mixcloud account on the internet. If you visit: www.mixcloud.com/markwheawill and follow me on there, you can listen back to the shows. There's also a Friday night Dance Music show including House, Trance and Drum N' Bass tracks which I recorded featuring lots of dance music anthems, hits and classics.

You'll be glad to know, despite all these major setbacks and after suffering from years of depression, I have recently started making and producing music again and rebuilding my second recording studio. I have got the enthusiasm and passion back for it all. I am much more wiser from my experiences and I have also re-launched my second record label which is called Uplifted Music. At the time of writing this book, my first new releases in over 12 years will be Mark Wheawill "Written in the stars" which is an instrumental House track and "Love will save the day" which is a catchy Trance record. Both records will be available on 12" vinyl and WAV format from the Uplifted Music & Media Portal Online Shop at www.upliftedmusic.co.uk. My music will just keep getting better and better!

I have also re-released my Vitality "Vitality" album on WAV format to celebrate the 14th anniversary since its original release on my first label TSYT RECORDINGS in 2004. It includes two bonus albums – "The White Album" and "The Black Album" which features 20 previously unreleased tracks and mixes which were written and produced around the time I wrote my first album. Some of these previously unreleased tracks and unheard mixes will be released on 12" vinyl and will be available to pre-order direct from the Uplifted Music & Media Portal Online Shop. Audio clips will be available to listen to on YouTube prior to their official release dates. I also hope to perform live at some gigs in the not too distant future if my hearing will permit it and collaborate with other artists.

I have also written a few other demo's and will be working on new tracks over the next year or so under my own name – Mark Wheawill and under new aliases such as "The Last Jedi". So, please keep an eye out for those new tracks and sign up to our newsletter and follow me on Instagram and Facebook. I also have a page on Facebook called "Music Industry Advice". I post regular tips and advice about the music business for musicians, artist and bands. I recommend you like and follow the page and if you ever require any advice, just send me a message on there, I'll be happy to help and I'll respond to you as soon as possible.

2018 and onwards will hopefully be the start of a new era. The next chapters in this book are designed to help you with your music career and provide you with a better understanding and insight into how everything works in the music industry. Even though I was unsuccessful in financial terms with regards to my music career, I was very successful in terms of output and number of official releases. This chapter has hopefully given you an insight into my life before I wrote this book and how I came to be at the stage where I am at now. This is how it all began.

So, I hope to continue where I left off in 2006. I see no reason to quit just yet and hang up my boots, so to speak. I have retired before from DJ'ing, but I believe I can still DJ on the radio without my hearing problems causing me too much hassle. A disability is not an inability. So, I will keep persevering and I hope you will too after reading this book! I hope it provides you with an enormous amount of inspiration. Just because I was unsuccessful in financial terms with my music as a result of not having a manager to look after my business affairs, does not mean my music was unsuccessful.

In fact, it was the complete opposite as you will have come to understand after reading this chapter. I relish a new challenge and I am determined as ever to carry on and prove all the haters and doubters wrong. I hope my new music will speak for itself and inspire many other musicians and other people in general with disabilities. I also hope to show people that you can bounce back from mental illness and depression. There is hope for the future. Just look at what Tyson Fury, the heavyweight boxer has achieved with his career in boxing!

I am also focused on running my record label - Uplifted Music and managing the Uplifted Music & Media Portal website and managing other artists and bands and helping market and distribute their music. I hope to improve conditions for artists and bands worldwide and change the negative attitudes and mentalities towards musicians in general. Artists should not be treated as unpaid slaves in the 21st century, that's for sure. I was always under the impression that slavery was abolished, but in the last few decades, this does not seem to be the case. Slavery seems to still exist. The world we live in is just an illusion.

It simply is not feasible and sustainable to work in the music industry in a voluntarily capacity anymore and running at a loss. If you're not a musician or involved in the music business and are reading this book out of curiousity, please help support musicians and help educate people as to the difficulties we face. It's always a constant struggle for the majority of artists. We need to be able to pay the bills and put food and drink on our tables at the end of the day. We do it for the love of the music, but we still have to remain realistic and get paid for our work and valuable contribution to the community.

2

MARKETING YOUR MUSIC IN THE 21st CENTURY

า an article published in an Australian online dance music magazine – Residentadvisor.net on eptember 1st 2004 in the Features section, I'd gone on record in an interview as saying "I'd like o work with the likes of Christina Aguilera and Kylie and create a whole new sound for them" in ıs so much words. It was in the same year that I released my debut album – Vitality "Vitality" on :D on my own record label – TSYT RECORDINGS. Not long before I ended up ill.

his article gained some unbelievable publicity for me. It found its way on to forums and other vebsites around the world in places as far away as Brazil, South America. It got everyone alking, especially fans of Christina Aguilera's from all over the globe! One famous reaction from ane of her fans on a forum which I will always remember was: "Who the hell is Mark Vheawill?". It wouldn't surprise me if the news got back to Christina herself and she said the ·xact same thing! I was still relatively unknown at the time and a rising star in the Progressive -louse/Trance music scene.

ıt the time, I was half joking and half being serious. I never thought it would actually get taken :o seriously and have the reaction that it did have. But hey, why not? Let's give it a try! Some ›eople viewed it as arrogance whilst some people were very positive and some of her loyal fans ›ooked forward to the idea of Christina creating a new style of music by fusing her vocals with Jance music. For me personally, I just saw it as self-belief and confidence in my abilities and an ıttempt to reach out to other artists who I admired and respected. I was in fact, a fan of :hristina Aguilera's music myself at the time and still am to this very day, so there didn't seem ıny harm in putting the word out there. I have all of Christina's albums except for "Bionic" vhich ironically was her dance music album that she released!

felt a strong connection with Christina and her music. That's the honest truth. It would have ›ecome another dream come true. After all, I was on a roll at the time with regards to my :lectronic dance music career and I was on the up. But at the same time, it kind of backfired on ne, big time! It ended up alienating me and everyone started acting differently around me from :hen on. Things have never quite been the same ever since! People just didn't seem to get my ıense of humour. Subsequently, I came up against severe control from the underground dance nusic scene and community and the record industry in general. I learnt a lot of lessons from :hat episode in my life. Make no mistake about that!

lust from those few comments in that article, I had engineered a piece of marketing genius. It ;ot my name out there and I still would like to work with her if I'm completely honest with you :specially after hearing her latest album "Liberation" which I believe is her best album to date ıs I write this chapter in July 2018. This example which I've used in this chapter helps to demonstrate the power of the internet and how you can market your music on a very low budget or with no marketing budget at all. Sometimes you just have to say what you want if it's within reach. At the same time though, you have to be realistic as well. I am under no illusion about that. Neither should you, dear reader!

Basically, the crux of the matter is that you need to get people talking about you and your music. You've got to give them something to talk about! Whether it's charity work you're doing or something you've done for the community, or something controversial or something that's really interesting. You need to be able to stand out from the crowd. The market is absolutely flooded with music these days since the internet has become much more popular and finding your music or people hearing about your music is like a needle in a haystack. You need to do that little bit extra and do something really special if you're not going down the traditional route of being signed to a major record label and getting exposure on TV and the radio and in the press in the way someone with a big marketing budget would do.

The key to a great marketing campaign and a successful marketing strategy is getting noticed by your target market. Take for example, the famous punk rock band - The Sex Pistols, who were credited for starting the punk movement. They sailed down the River Thames in London on a boat which they'd hired on the 7th June in 1977, whilst playing classic hits of theirs such as "Anarchy In The UK" and "God Save The Queen", as well as other songs and performed a surprise live gig which got them lots of media attention. It worked very well for them. You need to be original though and innovative. It's not always a good idea to copy other successful acts and marketing strategies that have been used before. They will not be as effective. You need to be doing something different. Otherwise, you'll be labelled as a copycat and people won't take as much notice and you will be less likely to stand out. The key here is originality in any marketing you do. The Sex Pistols were always very controversial and it did wonders for their career.

Also, take the band the Red Hot Chili Peppers for example. They created great publicity for themselves by playing at gigs naked wearing just socks on their private parts from 1983 and onwards. The band first made a name for themselves by doing their famous "socks on cocks" performance which they would continue doing for many years afterwards. This publicity stunt gained them massive exposure. It's stunts like these which help to launch artists and bands careers and put them in the media spotlight. It helps bring their music to the attention of the public. This is the kind of stuff you need to be doing to capture the public eye. If you don't come up with original ways of capturing people's attention, then chances are you will quickly fade into obscurity.

I remember when I went shopping in Warrington in England in the early-nineties, I walked past one of the record stores in the shopping precinct at the time and peered in and I noticed that there were a great deal of Oasis T-shirts in the shop window. At the time, I thought, who are Oasis? I'd never even heard of them or their music! Oasis were originally signed to Creation Records when they released their first album – "Definitely Maybe". Eventually, Oasis went on to be one of the biggest rock bands Britain has ever produced. Over 200,000 people attended their gigs at Knebworth in 1996 which made history and they were the largest outdoor concerts ever in the UK. Oasis were being marketed before they'd even released their debut album and had made it big. This proved to be a significant marketing strategy.

n the early noughties, I called myself a "Superstar DJ" in the third person on my own website at he time. I was an internet marketing guru at the time and no one else was giving me much redit for my superb DJ'ing skills and I thought why not, what harm can it do? This was meant as joke (I have a dry sense of humour as I've mentioned before) and as another publicity stunt ut it got taken seriously and I received a lot of stick off people within the electronic dance music scene and from other Progressive House/Trance music DJ's for having the nerve to do his. They were extremely jealous. But it wasn't like anyone was doing it for me and helping romote me, so in the end I had to do it myself. It's that old saying, "If you need a job doing, do yourself".

f anything, yet again, it alienated me but at the same time it was another piece of marketing enius. It got me loads of exposure. The hype worked! At the time when I was DJ'ing, the hype vas perfectly justified too because I knew how good I was on the old turntables. I think other eople have tried to do the same, but as it's been done so many times before, it is nowhere ear as effective to call yourself a "Superstar DJ" anymore. The public tend to decide for hemselves nowadays and there are thousands upon thousands of DJ's all competing for ttention using the same terms. Try calling yourself an "Inter-Galactic Superstar DJ"! Sorry, ou're too late. I've used that one myself too on social media very recently.

nyway, back to Christina Aguilera. Christina eventually went on to produce a new album called Bionic" without me. Surprise, surprise! I guess it was to be expected. I did end up ill not long fterwards as I explained in the first chapter of my book and the authorities tried to have me ectioned. So, that put an end to that dream for a while. Anything to discredit me I guess and nake me look crazy seemed to be the order of the day and objective by those in high places vhen I look back at the whole shenanigans. Those in power don't like outsiders muscling their vay in through the back door so to speak! I've always had a rebellious streak in me though. I am bit rock n roll.

lowever, maybe I can take some positivity out of that whole episode and take the credit for nspiring her to take a new direction with her music and playing around with electronic dance nusic sounds. I don't think "Bionic" was all that successful in terms of mass appeal and it was ot classed as one of her best albums. It's one of her albums which I don't own in my music :ollection and never bought. I may buy it eventually. Either way, I would still love to meet her ne day in the future and share stories about the music industry and still collaborate with her. 'm very interested to hear what she says about her song "Fall In Line". Anyway, I'm not retired ust yet! There's always hope and I am still entitled to dream. Life's about living your dreams sn't it? It's not the end of the world either if it never happens. What have you got to lose?

 must also add that, whilst I'm on this subject. I'm also keen on working with Taylor Swift and Kelsea Ballerini and producing one of their future albums or working on some tracks with them and working in the country music scene as I have been a big fan of country music ever since my :wo month stay in West Virginia in America in 2000. This time, I'm not joking either. I'm being deadly serious. Producing artists is what I love to do at the end of the day. I'm at home in a ecording studio. I like all these artists and their music a great deal. I'm a Record Producer.

That's my job and I'm always keen to work with established artists and bands and also new acts too.

If you never ask, you will never get to do the things you would like to do. What's the worst thing that can happen? They may reject me flat out. Or I may get criticized or receive a load of abuse! But I won't be losing any sleep over it though. We're only on this planet for a short time. There's no point going through life thinking "But what if?". So, don't hold back, but at the same time remember to be realistic about what goals you set for yourself. Make sure you do your groundwork first and foremost. If you are confident in your abilities and have the self-belief and can back it up, then anything is possible in this world. Dreams can come true for those who believe in themselves.

I fell in love with country music and that part of the world when I visited America and ended up watching the CMT (Country Music Television) channel in the motel that I was staying in for the duration of my two month stay, nearly every day and ended up buying a considerable number of albums on CD from the local Walmart store near to Princeton and Renick in West Virginia! I don't like to pigeonhole myself to just one genre of music either, especially when it comes to producing music. My taste in music is extremely varied and my collection of music that I have amassed over the years is very diverse. That's why I call the radio shows that I do - "Eclectricity" because they include an eclectic mix of music.

Unfortunately, though, country music doesn't get the same kind of exposure over here in the UK as it does in America. There is no dedicated Country music channel on TV here in the UK like there is in America with CMT. It's difficult to follow the scene due to this. If there was, our British music scene would be much better off and healthier for it as a result in my opinion. All you need to do is listen to songs like Faith Hill's "There will come a day" from her "Breathe" album and you will understand what I mean. Most of the music is about love. After all, music is the universal language. Country music certainly speaks to me, that's for certain.

Marketing in the 21st Century

Marketing has changed a lot over the last two decades. The emergence of the internet as a marketing tool has seen to that. A lot of artists and bands use social media in abundance now to reach out to their existing fans and new fans and it does work to an extent. But my only criticism is that the market is now flooded with people trying to get their music out there. It is starting to annoy people and come across as spam. The old, tried and tested ways do not work as effectively anymore. So, marketers are having to discover new ways of reaching out to audiences and fans to get their music heard. The internet is full of information but most people don't have enough time in the day to take notice of every advert or post on social media. You need to be more subtle with the way you market your music on the internet nowadays.

The music market is saturated with new artists and bands all trying to capture people's attention. There is so much clutter to wade through on social media such as Facebook and Instagram that it is becoming completely overwhelming. The amount of sponsored ads which keep popping up and appearing on social media without my consent is extremely off-putting. I end up spending far too much time sifting through all the junk that I'm not interested in. I really am not interested in discovering new artists and bands this way. I think this type of marketing strategy is very invasive and is very likely to have the opposite effect of what these artists and bands want. If anything it is making me start to use social media less and less. I believe that releasing quality music is one of the greatest marketing tools you can use. Just let fans find you and discover your music naturally. If it's meant to be, it will be!

This chapter on Marketing your music in the 21st century provides you with marketing strategies for marketing your music the D.I.Y (Do It Yourself) way. The D.I.Y approach is how I used to do it and how I market my music releases now. I don't know how large or small your marketing budget is, but in order to get your music out there and noticed, you need a marketing plan and you need to have a budget you can work with in order to implement your marketing plan and strategies. Marketing is creating a visible presence for your product/s. Whether it's marketing your music on the street, in a record store, on TV, on the Radio or in the Press, you need to get your music and you as the artist/s into the marketplace. That's what marketing is essentially.

I recommend that you start by concentrating on building up a fan base in your local vicinity or neighbourhood, then nationally and then internationally. Start off in small steps. Learn to walk before you start to run. Press up your own records yourself if you have to. Release your music on vinyl, CD and in WAV format. Physical copies of your music add value. I will tell you ways in which you can raise the funds to manufacture your music on to vinyl and CD in a later chapter if you don't have a record deal or lack the necessary means to do it yourself at the moment.

Forget about mp3's and streaming for the time being. Mp3's are of low quality and only devalue music and streaming only works for artists and bands that are signed to major record companies that get millions of streams and have licensing deals in place. They add no real value to your music. Streaming and low quality digital formats is ok as a promotional tool but as far as actually generating any royalties, it's useless in my opinion for independent artists and record labels. I will explain more about streaming later in this chapter and towards the end of my book and why I'm not keen on the whole idea of cloud based music.

You can utilize YouTube, Snapchat, Twitter, Facebook or Instagram as a promotional tool for your music releases by creating music videos for your music or short audio/video clips to gain exposure. Be creative. Capture your audience's attention. You don't need to spend fortunes on a music video to get your music noticed. You could do a live performance of your songs using Facebook Live, Twitch or a live video broadcast on Instagram. There are many tools you can use on the internet nowadays. These are just a few examples which I've listed. Use them all if you have to in order to increase coverage of your music and maximize your exposure on the worldwide web. The significant thing about using the web is that you can gain a global audience for your music without ever having to leave your home or the studio. Do not underestimate the power of the internet!

I would also advise you to get radio airplay by sending out promo copies of your music to all the appropriate radio stations, both online and offline that play your genre of music and participate in interviews so that fans can get to know you intimately. Put a street team together to help promote your music and give promo copies of your music to DJ's in the form of white label promos. It helps If DJ's include promos of your songs in their DJ mixes. It will help you get more attention. But remember to only send Third Parties low quality recordings of your music unless they license copies of music from you.

Try your best to obtain more publicity through features, articles, interviews and reviews of your music releases or live performances in the press such as magazines and newspapers. Also, place adverts in online and offline media outlets if your marketing budget will allow you to do so. Do a series of adverts if you can and work out which adverts are the most cost effective and which ones produce the best results by getting feedback from your fans. You will be able to work out which adverts to keep running in the press and which ones to stop doing.

Include your music videos on TV by networking with people in the broadcast industry. Advertise on TV channels if you can afford it and secure interviews on television. You may not be able to get featured on prime time television but all publicity is good publicity. If you do somehow manage to get on prime time TV, then you are either very lucky or you have the right contacts or you have an endless marketing budget. After all, networking is the way forward. TV is one of the most powerful mediums available to you in your arsenal of marketing tools. Remember this, it's not what you know, but who you know! It's the same with all aspects of life.

Put together a tour and do lots of live gigs to promote a single or album release. Make sure you have a banner at the back of the stage with your name or the name of your band on it, so that everyone knows who you are and remembers you. Create something visually aesthetic and pleasing to the eye on stage to keep your audience captivated. Whether that's a video in the background or people dancing on stage with you or a spectacular light show, it will help take your music and performances to another level.

Build relationships with your fans and the people in the industry who help you along the way. Keep in regular contact with everyone. Make sure you time everything right by creating a Marketing Calendar as part of your Marketing Plan and ensure that everything is coordinated to coincide with the release of your music on whichever formats you choose to release your music on or if you have any live gigs coming up.

Build an artist or band website which is dedicated to your act and your music and get listed on Google, Bing and all the other main search engines on the internet so that fans can find you or your website and create fan pages on social media so that your fans can connect with you and ask them to join your mailing list and send them a newsletter to keep your fans regularly updated with news of your future releases and forthcoming gigs and any other interesting bits of information. Don't overdo it though, otherwise you may scare some fans off and it may come across as spam!

Include a biography on your artist or band website and on your social media accounts. Tell your fans which artists have inspired you and who your music sounds like to give your audience an idea of what to expect. Use reviews of your music and gigs from any press publications and use quotes from any articles which you are featured in. It will help give you a lot more credibility. Remember to be original though. Your music needs to stand out from the crowd, so avoid sounding like a complete replica of another artist or band. Try to be unique. Try to be innovative and inspire the next generation of upcoming artists and bands. Go as far as creating your own sound that is instantly recognizable!

It would be advisable to perform at festivals and at private parties as another way of raising awareness of you and your music. Host your own house parties and invite some of your family, friends and fans along to meet you in person. Run competitions and give away some copies of your music, merchandise or tickets for free to see you perform live. Do the whole shebang. Do as many things as you can to maximize your reach potential and generate leads and turn them into lifelong fans of your music.

Performing and recording cover songs of other artists and band's music is an effective marketing strategy. It's one way of launching your career and getting a foot in the door and being noticed. It's probably not a good idea to cover songs which have been done many times before though. Instead, cover songs which haven't already been done! If You make a certain genre of music, this will help you to reach the right audience for your music and get your name out there. Consequently, potential fans may then decide to listen to more songs from your repertoire. You will also need to contact the artist or band who's song you are covering or their music publishing company for permission to use their songs in recordings or performances and ask for their permission to do this and strike up some deal with them.

Great album and single covers that are unique help to market music releases and contribute hugely to selling more copies of records. The artwork on the front of your album or single release can do wonders for artists and bands and can help grab people's attention. It can often make or break you. Especially, if it is iconic. There are many iconic album covers such as the Beatles "Sgt. Pepper's Lonely Hearts Club Band", Pink Floyd's "The Dark Side Of The Moon", Prince's "Purple Rain", The Smiths "Meat Is Murder", Nirvana's "Nevermind" and Guns N Roses "Appetite For Destruction". These are just a few of many examples I can think of. I highly recommend that you invest a lot of time and effort and put a lot of thought and energy into the creation of your single or album covers in order to appeal to consumers and capture their attention. Artwork plays a huge role in the marketing of music releases. It is not to be underestimated. You must consider the whole package when it comes to marketing your music!

Some artists and bands use marketing strategies which I would not advocate myself. They create the illusion of wealth and success which naïve fans often buy into. They do this through wearing expensive clothing and jewelry when they're out in public or in music videos or when being photographed by the paparazzi or media. They tend to use and drive flash cars in music videos or have pictures taken of themselves posing next to luxury cars. These are considered to be tricks of the trade to make them look more successful than they actually are. Rappers in particular are very guilty of this. It is often referred to as bling.

The best way to embrace the worldwide web is by building up a relationship with your fans. Relationship Marketing is the way forward in the 21st century. Let your fans into your lives. You don't need to show them your daily activities and routines, 24 hours per day and 7 days per week. You don't need to show them absolutely everything! Privacy comes first but when I say Relationship Marketing, I'm referring to building strong relations with your fans. Many artists and bands already do this now via social media. They broadcast live on Facebook and Instagram every now and again and communicate with their fans intimately and directly. Robbie Williams does it on Instagram as an example. He'll chat for a few hours whilst he's relaxing in a hotel or in-between gigs etc.

Sometimes, they'll perform a special live version of one of their songs or a few songs or an entire gig. You have to give something back to the fans. Your fans need to like you. This is very important. Whilst you're doing all of this, your fans are getting to know you more. Remember, we're here to entertain. We are in the entertainment industry. I believe this is one of the most important keys to effective marketing in the 21st century using the internet. You should embrace it, but don't overdo it to the point where you've not enough leisure time for yourselves. Otherwise you'll burn yourself out and end up ill with exhaustion.

You can do live question and answer broadcasts or posts on social media. Post regular pictures and videos and updates about your music, releases and live gigs. Show them a sneak peek into the recording of your next album. The more you do this, the stronger the bond with your fans. Get closer to your fans! I highly recommend you start doing this if you're not already doing it. A friend from the past told me that it's all about people liking you. It's not just about the music. It should be about the music alone, but it isn't unfortunately. Some people just like you as an artist or band for your music after listening to it, but some people want to get to know you better. It's the way of the world these days.

You don't have to do everything that revolves around your music. You can post all kinds of videos and pictures of your daily activities. A lot of fans like to see that you're a normal person too. They want to know who they're supporting and handing over their hard earned money to. Especially more so these days with the rising levels of corruption and greed within the music industry and record labels and third party streaming services and download sites not paying the artists at all or very rarely, in some cases. They need to see that you are genuine and entertaining. It is no different to a fan following one of their close friends on social media. People want to be entertained!

You can also run competitions on social media and give away free promotional copies of your music or tickets to see you in concert. You can take pictures of you with your fans and post them on your social media accounts like country music artists - Taylor Swift and Kelsea Ballerini do. UK artist - Ellie Goulding posts videos and pictures about her environmental work and campaigns which she does to help raise awareness of important issues in the world such as using less plastic and disposing of it more properly. Show your fans your caring and kind hearted side by videographing the charity work which you do. Show your fans that it's not about the money and that you do it for the love. This will all have a much bigger impact on your relationship with your fans and will help you to get more fans too.

I suggest you record all kinds of footage of you or your band working on new songs, rehearsing, jamming and improvising in the studio and also post these on your social media accounts. You can also give fans an exclusive insight into the creation of your music videos and tour productions. There are so many things you can do. A lot of which has been done before but I'm sure you can come up with many original ideas of your own which haven't been covered by any other artists or bands. The secret is being as creative and innovative as possible and doing groundbreaking things.

It's not just about the music these days, it's also about what you do or can do for the community. The aim isn't necessarily to gain more fans, it's to demonstrate that you are human. It's all about having something in common with your audience and finding ways in which you can connect with your fans. Some artists and bands get involved in politics. I wouldn't recommend doing this as you are just as likely to lose fans as well as gain new fans, but only the brave ones should do this. If you really feel passionate about a certain issue, then by all means go for it, but it's not always a good idea to mix politics with music as I have found through my own experiences.

US artist - Kaya Jones (once of the Pussycat Dolls) gets regularly involved in politics and I respect her greatly for this but I know she has lost a lot of fans as a result of this. The famous grunge band Pearl Jam also do it. Sometimes it puts people off as we all have different views on things and don't always see eye to eye or we can't always agree on the same thing. It's risky business, that's for sure! But in modern times, some of us feel the urge and necessity to air our opinions on social media and get deeply involved in it all. Especially with what's going on in the world in these last two decades. It takes very bold people to do this. I guess it's our pedestal. However, for some, it can spell an end to their music careers. You have to ask yourself, what is more important? Is it a risk worth taking? I personally believe that you just have to do what you feel is right and to listen to your heart.

I'm always constantly expressing my opinions on serious matters on social media and I am not afraid to do so. If it means sacrificing a music career in the name of doing what's right, then so be it. I've lived most of my dreams already, so I've nothing to lose! But if you're new to the music business and just starting out, it could be career suicide for you. So, please think carefully before you do anything and take time to consider everything before you press that submit button on your social media accounts.

Niche Marketing

Another method of marketing which not many artists and bands use is Niche Marketing. Most people tend to copy other acts or make music in the style of pre-existing genres and sub-genres of music. Not many artists and bands ever consider making their own style of music. It's a lot easier to market your music in an already pre-existing genre or sub-genre of music but it's also possible to get a bigger market share if you make music that hasn't been done before. Niche markets are the best place to start if you want to be really successful and grab the attention of record labels and the publlc.

I recommend you make niche music if you want to get anywhere in the music business. It's easier to take a slice of the pie making niche music than it is making music that many artists and bands already make and which is available in abundance. You have more competition otherwise. For example, if you create a new sub-genre of music or start a new scene or movement and become a pioneer in that genre, you are more likely to increase your sales. Just look to the punk scene and electronic dance music scene as examples. These new genres and sub-genres of music started new movements and were very successful. Everything else has been done to death!

It is better to be a pioneer and innovator than it is to copy others. If you are the first to do something, then chances are people will buy your music or any product or service for that matter. It may not be as easy to market your music if a new style of music is created, but you will obtain a bigger slice of the pie. It is much better to produce original new music than to copy everyone else. That's the best advice I can give you in this chapter. Start a new movement. Grab the attention of all the major record companies and they will soon come knocking at your door offering you all kinds of deals.

What people don't realize is that if you want to be really successful in the music business, you have to go through their channels. This means signing to their record companies and only a few get signed up and are really successful. But if you're making a new type of music that's never been covered before, then chances are you are more likely to get signed up or get noticed by fans who want something fresh and innovative and to hear something different than they've heard before. Make groundbreaking new music and you will be remembered for an eternity!

You will also receive a lot more recognition for starting a new movement. You will become legends in your own right. You will be the founding fathers of a new genre or sub-genre of music. The list of benefits is endless. People will talk about you through word of mouth and will write about you in books. They will produce documentaries about you and your music. This is the best form of advertising known to man. They will also have to create new categories of music in record stores and on music portals and magazines will have to devote entirely new review sections to review your genre of music. Does Niche Marketing not seem more appealing to you now that I've listed all these crucial advantages? Or would you prefer to carry on struggling for the rest of your life competing with every other artist and band who creates rock or rap music etc.?

I personally take the credit for creating new sub-genres of electronic dance music in the Progressive House music scene. I was the first to create "Future House" and "Space Funk" sub-genres of music with my "Future House Mix" of a track I made called "Transition" which was released on Baroque Records back in 2003 under my own name – Mark Wheawill. I also did a remix of the same record called the "Space Funk Vocal Mix" which was never officially released but it was available on the underground circuit. I'm not advocating that everyone should go out and start making new genres or sub-genres of music, but you will find it much more easier getting your music out there if it's not been done before. You are just a needle in a haystack otherwise amongst an ocean of music.

If you want to be truly successful, you need to be one step ahead of the rest all the time, not just for the time being, but always! It's the only way to have longevity in the music business. You need to be forward thinking. These tips and advice which I am giving you are genuine and I really do want to help you succeed in the music industry. It's no good copying everyone else. It just gets boring and stale. You are also more likely to succeed if you keep reinventing yourself and the music which you produce. I advise you to play the game if you want to stand out from the crowd and be a huge success.

Underground Marketing

There are also ways in which to market your music on an underground level. I call this type of marketing – "Underground Marketing". If you are struggling to get your music in to all of the major retailers such as HMV and Walmart and on online retailers such as ITunes and Amazon etc. Then, I would recommend that you organize tours and put on gigs and sell your music at the venues on CD, Vinyl and WAV formats. You can either press up a few thousand copies on each format and then sell your music direct to your fans at each gig and cut out all the middlemen or you could provide fans with pre-order forms which they can fill in at the venue and accept payments from them, there and then and issue them with a receipt or they could take the order forms home with them and then send them off to you at a later date and make payment or alternatively, they could visit your online shop (Music Portal) and pre-order your music from there.

I believe that the best way forward in this day and age is to have your own form of retail outlet/s. You can achieve this by having your own online shop in the form of a Music Portal very much like my Music Portal at www.upliftedmusic.co.uk which I will discuss further with you and talk about more extensively in Chapter 6. You need a tangible product to sell on a Music Portal which fans can order. So, you need to make albums and singles and then do gigs to promote the music releases and build up a strong fan base. If you do not have the capacity to create your own Music Portal, the other alternative is to get your music releases stocked on a sale or return basis on other Music Portals or on Pre-Order only in order to sell your music direct to your fans and cut out all the unnecessary middlemen.

In order to help promote your music releases, you need to get airplay on the radio and create music videos for each single release which will help promote your album/s. These are the main things which you need to do in order to launch an effective marketing strategy without relying on too many third parties and greedy middlemen. Having a tangible product or products is much better than selling your music as a digital download or on streaming services. There is no money in digital downloads and streaming unless you have licensing deals in place. Digital is only really effective as a promotional tool as I've mentioned before.

It is also possible to start your own Distribution Company and reach a deal with retailers and get your music stocked in their stores or on their download and streaming services through doing the distribution yourself. Retailers tend not to deal direct with artists and bands and record labels because of the workload that is involved in accounting to everyone. The other solution would be to start your own online shop or Music Portal as I call them. Or you could approach an existing Music Portal and ask them to stock your music on a sale or return basis if you have pressed up so many copies of your music and would like to get rid of them as soon as possible. You could also let the Music Portal take pre-orders on your behalf which would prevent surplus copies being pressed up and would reduce a lot of the financial risks involved with manufacturing music on to CD, Vinyl and WAV formats.

If you are also finding it difficult to get gigs and find venues willing to let you perform live, you could hire a truck and take a portable sound system with a generator and huge speakers and perform live gigs at impromptu street parties and air your music that way. If the response is positive, you could hand out flyers with information about you or your band and links to your online shop or website and then you could release a single and sell it direct to your fans. This is one way of building a fan base and getting noticed. It is very much the same concept as illegal raves or house parties. It's an underground way of reaching your audience.

Another proposal would be to perform a gig on the high street in a busy or crowded shopping centre/mall in a similar way to busking. You could perform an acoustic version of a few of your songs and hand out flyers with information on them about your music to passersby. This would be a really effective way of marketing your music and reaching out to people and hopefully gaining new fans. I saw a clip of Christina Aguilera on one of her Instagram posts doing the same thing in a subway in New York in America recently. She wore a disguise and the crowd that had gathered to watch the performance were in complete awe and shock when they realized who was performing. It's little things like these which gets people talking and helps gain publicity.

You could also start up your own radio station (online/offline or both) as a way of getting your music heard. Radio stations receive a plethora of music from record labels and artists and bands and generate massive revenue streams from advertising income. There is nothing to stop entrepreneurial artists and bands doing the same. Not only would you have control over what music gets discovered by the public but you could also generate additional revenue streams. You can start your own group or company and buy up pre-existing radio stations if you have a few million pounds to spare or start your own radio station from scratch. Alternatively, you could take the cheaper option and start up your own internet radio station as a way of getting your music aired. These are all great ways of overcoming any obstacles or hurdles that may come your way which happens often in the music industry.

As another suggestion, you could open up your own branch of independent record stores on the high street and stock your music in them. This would take a lot of team work of course and you'd need a fair bit of money behind you to make it a reality. There are always solutions to the many problems we face and there are so many ways to market your music in the 21st century that there isn't enough room in this book to tell you about them all. I suggest you do a lot of research and read a lot of marketing books and watch a lot of videos and ask people in the music business for tips and advice. I am also available to help you with marketing your music on a freelance basis, so please don't be afraid to get in contact with me and ask for my help. I relish the challenge! I am positive I can come up with solutions to your problems in such challenging times.

Recap

Below is a recap of everything I have discussed in this chapter and a list of all the marketing tools you can use to give your music more chance of exposure (I have used examples of both British and International outlets):

Promotion – Inclusion of your music on playlists

- YouTube
- Spotify (I wouldn't recommend putting your music on Spotify though!)
- Apple Music
- Supermarkets
- Gyms
- On-Hold Playlists (for Customer Service queues on the phone)

Promotion – Advertising

- Word Of Mouth
- Affiliates (Commission on Sales of Music & Merchandise)
- Referrals
- Web Forums
- Blogs
- Vlogs
- Podcasts
- RSS Newsfeeds
- Artist/Band Website

- Newsletters

- Email Marketing Campaigns

- Social Media Posts –
  Facebook/Twitter/Instagram/Google+/Pinterest/LinkedIn/Snapchat/Twitch

- Instagram TV

- Instagram Stories

- Facebook Live

- Myspace

- Reverbnation

- Competitions (Free Promo Giveaways)

- Facebook Messaging

- Whatsapp Messaging

- Twitter Messaging

- Mobile Phone/Cellphone Messaging

- Audio/Video Clips
  (YouTube/Vimeo/Facebook/Twitter/Instagram/Google+/Snapchat/Musical.ly)

- White Label Promo Copies (To give to DJ's and Radio Stations)

Promotion – In the Press and on various Media both Online and Offline

- Magazines

- Newspapers

- TV

- Radio

Promotion – Visible presence on stage and Merchandise you can sell at Gigs

- Banners (at the back of the stage)

- Lighting

- Videos (at the back of the stage)

- Dancers

- Pyrotechnics

- Flyers

- Posters (Signed and Limited Edition)

- T-Shirts

- Caps

- Hoodies

- Flags

- Bags

- Fridge Magnets

- Coffee Mugs

- Mouse Pads/Mats

- Keyrings

- Pens

Promotion – Promotional Gigs and Appearances at Record Stores

- Photographs (Meet and Greet Fans)

- Signing T-Shirts

- Signing CD's/Vinyl/Cassettes

- Signing Posters

- Live Performances

Distribution – Getting your music into Shops/Stores and on Online Music Retailers

- HMV

- Sainsbury's

- Asda/Walmart

- Tesco

- ITunes

- Amazon Music

- Independent Record Shops

- Your own Record Shops

- Online Music Portal (Take online orders for physical formats i.e. CD's, Vinyl, Cassette, WAV)

- Third Party Music Portals (Sale or return or Pre-Orders)

- Ringtones

Distribution – Underground Retail

- Gigs (Sell Music/Merchandise at gigs)

- House Parties

- Affiliates

- Music Portals

Methods of Marketing

I have listed other marketing tools which you can use below. I would advise you to read up on the different methods of marketing strategies which you can use or watch videos about these types of marketing and decide which apply to you and to the music business:

- 80/20 Marketing

- Relationship Marketing

- Niche Marketing

- Underground Marketing

- Permission Marketing

- Email Marketing

- Digital Marketing

- Influencer Marketing

- Attraction Marketing

- Network Marketing

- Guerilla Marketing

- Viral Marketing

- Fusion Marketing

- You Marketing

- Combination Marketing

- Intelligent Marketing

- Cause-Related Marketing

- Social Media Marketing

- E-Commerce

I hope this chapter will give you a head start in your quest to make it in the music business. If you cover all of the marketing strategies which are listed in this book and available to you, you will have more chance of being successful. Remember this, the most important marketing tool you have in your arsenal of marketing tools is your music itself. If you make and release quality music that fans like, then the music will do the talking for itself. You won't even need to market it!

I wish you all the best and if you ever need any help or assistance, I will be glad to be of service to you. Now you have a fairly good idea of how to market yourself and your music, the next step is actually selling your music. Selling your music is the most difficult part. It's not as easy as you think! In the next chapter, I address this particular subject and I discuss ways in which to sell your music in the 21st century.

3

HOW TO SELL YOUR MUSIC IN THE 21st CENTURY

Traditionally, record labels have always pressed up thousands, hundreds of thousands and millions of copies of records for each album release and then physically distributed them to retailers all over the world. They'd flood the market with millions of copies of a record so that there was no escaping a certain artist or bands visible presence in each record store on the high street and it was very difficult to avoid the sight of an album in say HMV or Virgin Megastore in the UK. This in itself was a great marketing strategy during those times. Nowadays though, with the decline in record sales on CD and vinyl in the last two decades, it doesn't make good business sense to do this anymore due to the development of the worldwide web and digital downloads and streaming services.

Artists such as Jessie J with her single release "Price Tag" which was released in 2011 and band like Radiohead with their "pay what you want" ethos helped ruin the music industry as we used to know it. It started a chain reaction with Jessie J's "We don't need your money" lyrics in her h song "Price Tag" amongst the general public and created a "money doesn't matter" type of attitude towards artists and bands and people got the impression that we could just do it completely voluntary. This played right into the public's hands and they started to expect music for free and to never really have to pay for it. We were all being played by the music industry and the public so that they didn't have to stick their hands in their pockets and pay for goods anymore.

Jessie J and Radiohead as well as many other artists and bands don't have a clue about the business side of the music industry. No of course we're not in it for the money. We do it because we love making music and performing live. It's our passion! But let's be realistic about this. It costs time and money to make and record music, release it and promote it and to put gigs on. Not to forget the hundreds or thousands of hours spent learning our crafts when we were younger. People seem to forget this and take it all for granted. They simply do not have a clue about the amount of time we invest and the vast sums of money that go into making, releasing and promoting records on a global scale. We need to have some common sense about all of this. We all need to eat and drink and pay the bills. We simply cannot afford to do it solely for the love of it in a voluntary capacity and never earn a living. It just isn't feasible unless certain artists and bands are aristocracy and are rich to begin with. Then, that would make sense and explain their attitudes.

However, as people involved in the music industry are starting to realize there is no money in digital downloads and streaming. Unless you're the streaming service or a major record company or a superstar. Digital music adds no real value to music. It is nothing more than a cheap promotional tool. Yes, it has great potential to reach a worldwide audience and reduce overheads for record companies and independent artists. They no longer need to spend thousands, hundreds of thousands and millions of pounds or dollars on manufacturing records. But this is the problem you see. There are less overheads, but yet artists and bands are still suffering when it comes to getting paid for their work.

Fear not all you guys and girls who are traditionalists. Vinyl, CD and Cassette formats are starting to make a significant comeback! Giant supermarkets in the UK such as Sainsbury's and independent record stores are starting to stock more vinyl records and CD's. The retro formats are making a big revival. This is great news for all musicians, the public and the music industry as a whole! This means we get the best of both worlds. Those who prefer the old formats can still buy music on their favourite physical formats and the younger generations who have grown up with and taken to digital downloads and streaming can carry on listening to music and purchasing music online or they have the choice of converting to CD and vinyl. Right now, they know no different. The younger generations don't really know what they're missing.

Vinyl and CD formats are much better quality than digital downloads and streaming. The standard of the audio is much more superior whereas mp3 and streaming is inferior compared to their old predecessors. Vinyl has a distinctive warmer sound to it because it is pure analog. I believe this is what is so much more appealing to music fans. This is why it is starting to make a resurgence. People are starting to realize that analog actually sounds better than digital. I understand that vinyl scratches very easily and can melt in the sun, but if you look after your records carefully, then there will be no problems.

It may take another five to ten years for Vinyl and CD formats to get back to the sales levels they used to be at before the digital revolution. But I believe with my whole heart that these formats and WAV format will become increasingly popular over the next decade. We have to embrace the future but that's no excuse to dump past technologies which worked so well before. It was the problem with file-sharing that started all this back in the early noughties. Napster was to blame partly for that. The music industry became insecure and very paranoid whilst consumers started to expect music for free.

Now it would seem there is a move towards getting fans to pay more money in the long term for music releases via a pay-per-play scheme and business model. The music industry no longer want fans to own copies of records. They are encouraging people to rent music as opposed to owning it. It's happening with lots of industries that sell software. The jukebox of the old days seems to be the answer to their problems. The likes of Spotify are the jukebox of the 21st century. The younger generations seem to be happy to go along with this but I don't think they truly understand what's happening. It's a conundrum. They believe they are getting value for money and access to a vast catalogue of music. But all is not what it seems. I will speak about this more later on this chapter.

Do we really need middlemen in the music industry anymore?

In the days of old, to release music you needed to sign a record deal with a record company. The record company would then get your music pressed on to vinyl or CD or tape cassette and would then use a distribution company to distribute your music and get it into the retailers stores on the high street such as Woolworths, HMV and Virgin Megastores. Music had to be physically distributed because it was only available on physical and tangible formats. Music releases also took up valuable storage space in warehouses before it was distributed to record stores by men and women in trucks and vans and then it took up valuable shelf space in the stores which all the major record companies and independents competed vigorously for. It wasn't always easy to get a record deal and get your music stocked in the prestigious record stores at the time and most independent record labels and artists and bands would opt for getting their music in to the backstreet independent record stores instead as a way of getting their music out there.

With the rise of the internet and digital goods, the need for distributors has started to diminish. Music doesn't necessarily need to be physically distributed anymore due to the increasing demand for music on streaming formats and digital downloads delivered instantly to your desktop computer, laptop, tablet or mobile/cell phone devices. There are a lot less costs involved in manufacturing music now and distributing it. So, people don't want to spend loads of money on music anymore to get it to consumers. Therefore, why are we using distributors to distribute our music to digital music content platforms such as ITunes, Amazon Music and Spotify, when we can do it ourselves? Wouldn't it make more sense for us to distribute our own music or start our own digital distribution companies and take care of that side of the business ourselves?

I must also mention as an important point for you to remember, if you only anticipate selling a few thousand copies of your records if you're still dealing in physical formats, then there's no point going through loads of middlemen such as record labels, distributors and retailers. You'll end up with a lot less income from royalties from sales of your records and it won't be enough to share with everyone and pay all your bills. So, the less people that are involved in the process, the better it is for you in the long term. This is only if you don't mind selling a few hundred or a few thousand copies of your records and doing all the extra work yourselves. Surely, it's worthwhile if it means getting paid for your work?

The only reason you need to be selling hundreds of thousands or millions of copies of your records is because there are more mouths to feed. This is the reasoning behind why superstars exist in the music business. The likelihood is that there are thousands of people around the globe working as a team to help promote a certain act and this is why they become so famous. These particular acts become mainstream brands and receive the backing of many institutions on account of the number of people involved in a project. There is a need to sell a lot more copies of an artist or band's music due to this factor.

This is a real insight into the music industry for you. If you're an independent artist or band, you only really need a minimum of a few thousand fans to sustain a career in the music business and earn a living. But if you're signed to a major record company and have a huge team supporting you and backing you, then you will need to sell a lot more copies. In fact, you will need to sell hundreds of thousands or millions of copies of your records worldwide to pay everyone else's salaries. There will be a lot more pressure on you to perform to your best abilities and to produce the results that everyone desires. It is much more difficult to earn a living from music if you're an independent artist as you don't have the support, financial backing and team behind you like an artist or band signed to a major record label.

However, there's less pressure on you as an independent artist and you don't have to worry about feeding everyone. You only need to worry about feeding yourself and your small inner circle. You don't necessarily need to be in the limelight or become famous or a superstar either. But, when you're signed to a big label, there's an enormous amount of burden on you to perform and be successful and for you to be a recognizable star. Do you really want to be recognized everywhere you go? There are many side effects to being a famous artist or a superstar such as attracting bad energy or becoming addicted to drugs or developing mental health problems etc. So, think carefully about what you want from your music career. You have to be a really strong character to survive the music business and stardom.

How do you gauge success? Well, if you're happy to struggle along and sell a few thousand records, then surely it can be seen as a success. Whereas if you're having to sell millions of copies of your music, then there is going to be a hell of a lot more pressure on you and success will only come if you can feed everyone who's involved in supporting you along the way. Otherwise, a major record company will soon drop you from their roster if sales aren't performing how they'd expect them to. If you don't want fame and fortune, then the independent route is the best way forward for you and you can do your own distribution. If you don't mind fame, fortune and stardom and work well under extreme pressure, then a major record deal is more suited to you. You'll have more time to focus on making music and can leave the distribution to someone else. My only advice on this subject is to be careful what you wish for!

So, if you're only planning on selling digital music or pressing up a few thousand copies of your music on Vinyl and CD formats, then you may as well do the distribution yourself and then, there will be more chance of getting paid for your music. But if you're selling hundreds of thousands or millions of copies of your records on physical formats, then you're much better off doing a deal with a distribution company and getting them to help distribute your music due to the workload that is involved. There is still a need for distributors and involving middlemen, but as far as distributing digital music online, there is no real need for third party distribution companies anymore or aggregators as they sometimes call them.

There is no requirement for record companies either if they're not financing the recording of your music anymore and if they're not willing to pay you for the right to exploit your music (your intellectual property) and there is no need for download stores, streaming services and online shops if you can bypass them and sell your music direct to the fans yourself. There is no need for so many middlemen in the 21st century. Not when you can sell music direct to your fans. The more people involved in the whole marketing and sales process, the less money there is to go around after everyone else has taken their cut. This is the main reason why artists rarely get paid. The greedy and selfish middlemen have always helped themselves to the slices of the pie first. There are no slices left for the artist by the time they've finished. So, you have to take the slices of the pie first and cut all the middlemen out if you want to eat!

If you're not bothered about becoming a star or becoming famous, and you are happy and content with a few thousand fans, then sell your music direct to them and cut out as many middlemen as you can and you will still earn a decent living and you will be able to continue making music and playing live. Start your own record label, do your own distribution and start your own retail store. Do everything in-house and sell direct to your fans. If you don't have the time to do everything yourself, then work together with other people but keep that circle of people small so that everyone gets paid and everyone has a slice of the pie.

If it's stardom you want and you want to become a superstar, then you will need to work as part of a massive team. You will need a big record company behind you helping to exploit your music, you will need a distributor to help distribute your music and you will need to get your music in as many retailers as possible. So, in this scenario, middlemen are inevitable. Just make sure you sign a contract that benefits you in the long term and ensures you get paid a regular salary, so you can pay all your bills and eat and drink and to be able to live comfortably and afford everything you need. Don't sign any bad deals and get screwed over. Make sure you get a slice of the pie too!

The trouble with cloud based music

As I write this book, cloud based music is becoming more and more popular with fans of music. YouTube are just starting to introduce a subscription based model for streaming music from their new app and Spotify and Apple Music are making serious money from their streaming services. Spotify recently floated on the stock market and currently have about 83 million subscribers according to the latest reports. Not only have they made a huge amount of money from selling shares to investors, but they also charge subscription fees and generate further income streams from advertising revenue. Spotify are making serious money but most artists are still finding it difficult to get paid if at all.

More and more streaming services are popping up by the day. However, no one has stopped to think about the implications of this new trend. The real beneficiaries from this new business model are streaming services such as Spotify and only the internet service providers (ISP's) and telecommunication companies will benefit from streaming by encouraging people to use more of their data allowances on their mobile/cell phones etc. This is yet another industry scam. Both artists and fans stand to lose out. Trust me on this, I'm an expert in this field.

Cloud based music is not the answer! It merely serves as a cheap promotional tool at best. Have you ever wondered what will happen if the internet goes down? If the internet ever goes down, no one will be able to listen to music online as it will all be cloud based. DJ's will not be able to play and promote music releases either. How do we expect our music to ever receive maximum exposure if DJ's can't play and promote the music? DJ's are crucial to the whole process of promoting music. It is of my opinion that streaming is not a viable platform. It's not the solution to musicians problems. It's an additional promotional tool, but that's about all it is.

For a start, the audio quality of streamed music is not as good as vinyl, CD or WAV format. Streamed audio is inferior! It's also not a tangible product which fans can hold in their hands and play when they feel like it and read through the inlay card and the lyrics to sing along to their favourite tunes and examine the artwork which comes along with the whole package of a release. It also makes no economic sense whatsoever. It will cost fans more money to listen to music this way in the long term than buying music releases on CD, vinyl or WAV format due to increased charges for data allowance packages and using up all their data allowance on their mobile/cell phones! Fans are basically renting the music as opposed to owning copies which is a bad deal for consumers.

Instead of making a one off payment to buy a copy of a music release on CD or vinyl, fans will keep having to pay to listen to the music and still never own a copy for the rest of their lives. This is a really bad deal for both creators of music and fans alike. Gone are the days when fans could own a copy of their favourite artist and band's music it seems. Most people in the music industry are following suit and copying this business model believing it to be the answer to their problems. I disagree, I genuinely believe this is not the way to go. This is not the way forward. How do you expect people to listen to your music if it is only cloud based and fans can't access the internet?

Not everyone has access to the worldwide web. Shops on the high street will go out of business and people will lose their jobs. There will be no independent record stores. There will be no face to face contact with the company you are buying the music from. Artists and bands will just get screwed over even more. I can see where this is all leading to. I can see the problems and issues which will arise as a result of musicians relying on cloud based music instead of manufacturing tangible products. Physical goods add more value to music whereas digital products devalue music.

Has anyone ever stopped to have a think and thought about the consequences of having cloud based only music? Have you ever wondered what would happen if the internet goes down permanently or temporarily and the havoc this would cause for fans, the music industry and the creators of music if we were to go completely digital and cloud based? I don't think people have thought this one through properly! All the music stored on the servers of streaming servers could become inaccessible or the worst case scenario could be that music is lost forever.

If there is a problem with your internet connection, you will not be able to listen to music or play it. If your internet service provider (ISP) has a problem and you have no internet access, again, you will not be able to listen to the music you have subscribed to. If there is an issue with satellites out in space or internet cables on the bottom of ocean floors, you will not be able to listen to the music you have paid for. Is this an acceptable price to pay for having only cloud based music? Has anyone ever considered any of these points? If you have a turntable or CD player you can just play your music without having to worry about internet outages. With cloud based music there is no independence and fans of music are completely dependent on the telecommunications companies and ISP's.

I would not recommend dumping physical formats and just relying on cloud based music. It is best to have the best of both worlds. Utilize everything and cover all angles and give fans the choice as to what formats they want to listen to music on. This is why I refuse to go along with the herd. I am not a sheep following the herd. I can think for myself and I am not influenced by sheep. I can see into the future and I envisage all the potential problems with cloud based music. Yes, I agree it's a cheap way of getting your music out there on a global scale and a good promotional tool. But that's all it is. It serves no other real purpose. If you have no access to the music you've paid for and subscribed to on these streaming services, how do you play the music? How do you play it to your family and friends? How do you play it to your children if you don't own a copy on CD or vinyl etc.?

I anticipate all the pitfalls of this new technology and cloud based music business model. If you choose to ignore my advice on this matter, then that is completely up to you. You will be making a huge mistake and will live to regret not covering all formats. I am doing the sensible thing and choosing to ignore the so called current trend and do what I believe to be the best way forward in the long term for my music and for all artists and bands who release music on my own record label - Uplifted Music and for all music available to buy from the Uplifted Music & Media Portal Online Shop. I choose to sell music both online and offline and keep the traditional record stores alive and keep people in employment. It's much better for the economy. I don't want to deal with faceless corporations like Spotify or distribution companies. I am trusting my gut instinct and using my brains this time. I know how to go about selling music in the 21st century. I know how to make sure artists and bands get paid for their work.

It makes perfect sense to retain the traditional business models that have worked perfect for decades and visit record stores to buy music on vinyl, CD and future physical mediums and speak to someone face-to-face and buy music releases in person. It's what humans need. We need social interaction. You just don't get that with streaming music and downloading it. Where is the fun in streaming music? How else do you socialize with other fans of music in the flesh if you never visit a record store and only stream music from streaming services? No one seems to understand the human psyche. They are missing these vital points! The social aspect of music is one of the most important parts of being a fan of music. It's all about the community and building communities. It's part of the reason why people love going out and going to gigs. There's nothing natural about streaming music. Where is the human element to it all? The machines seem to be taking over!

I suggest that you cover all the various formats if you want to be truly successful with regards to selling your music and give fans plenty of choice. Let them decide what formats they want to use but educate them on the disadvantages of cloud based music and all the risks attributed with just streaming music. Cloud based music on its own is a bad move and fans will discover that it is costing them more of their disposable income in the long term. When all the technical problems start to arise, there will be uproar and there will be a lot of frustrated music fans when they realize the downsides involved with playing music online and didn't see the drawbacks of this new format.

here will be outrage as they didn't foresee the potential problems that come with cloud based nly music and they will have major regrets. The music industry don't even seem to know what ney're doing the majority of the time and they don't seem to understand the full implications f cloud based only music. I think they are confused and they don't understand all the technical argons. It is very foolish to dump the formats that worked so well in the past. The only people nat stand to benefit from streaming in the short term is the streaming services themselves and ne telecommunication companies and ISP's. When music fans recognize that they are being ipped off and given a bad deal, this will lead to an increase in demand for physical goods again nd a return to the traditional formats that worked best in the decades before. I'm a million per ent certain of this! So, get ready for a rapid return to physical formats and new physical nediums such as WAV format on USB Flash Drives. I'm already leading the way!

: is also advantageous to supply music releases direct to fans via Music Portals on all of the hysical formats which fans can own and play and listen to whenever they like, and cut out the reedy middlemen who serve no real purpose in the music industry such as third party digital nusic aggregators and digital distributors. Digital music distribution is done autonomously and here is no real work involved and no justification for the fees which they charge record labels nd creators of music. They are just middlemen and another step in the process to getting paid or your music. They just want a big slice of the pie for very little work.

f you want to make money from streaming you need to license your music to the streaming ervices and demand an advance licensing fee upfront and then monthly, quarterly or yearly censing fees (whichever suits you best). Do not rely on royalties from number of streams/plays is you will be shortchanged and you will end up extremely disappointed when you receive your ales statements. Licensing your music to third party digital music content platforms such as potify will ensure that you get paid.

'ou should be receiving payments from these streaming services irrespective of how many treams/plays or downloads you are getting as this cloud based music business model is open to orruption and abuse. It will safeguard your best interests in the long term. Please remember nat these streaming services are basically digital music jukeboxes and nothing more or nothing ess. So, charge them accordingly and bear in mind the risks associated with streaming, otherwise you and fans of your music are in for a big shock in the future and will end up isenchanted.

Pre-Orders

he way to sell your music in the 21st century on physical formats is to start taking pre-orders only for your music releases. This helps to save you a lot of money with regards to manufacturing, pressing and duplication costs and reduces your overheads massively and you are less likely to end up in serious debt or go bankrupt. There is no need to take big risks anymore and press up more copies than you need to. There is little point in pressing up say 10,000 copies of your music on Vinyl, only to sell 1,000 copies and be left with 9,000 surplus copies taking up important storage space. You might not even be able to give away copies of your music.

This new business model will help reduce waste and expense. By just taking pre-orders only, you can gauge exactly how many copies of a record to press up on to Vinyl format and CD before you officially release your music to the public. This is the solution to all of our problems and it is also a much more environmentally friendly way of doing it. The oil companies want you to press up hundreds of thousands or millions of Vinyl records or CD's as it makes them super rich no matter how many copies you sell or not. It's a win-win situation for them if you press numerous copies of your music up on to physical formats. But if you do it on a pre-order only basis, then it is a win-win situation for you and for the environment and the planet in general! Planet Earth is more likely to love us and there will be a lot less pollution.

You can take pre-orders online on websites (online shops/music portals), at gigs and in record stores. All you need to do is create an online form which customers can fill in or a paper form in record stores or at gigs and fans can pay months in advance of an official release date and there is less chance of having surplus copies of records leftover which you can't sell or giveaway. This method of practice will be much more efficient than ever and help keep many record labels afloat; independent artists and bands will have longevity in the music business and it will improve their chances of success. What's the point of pressing up a million copies of a record and then only being able to shift a hundred thousand copies? It makes no sense whatsoever to continue doing it this way, especially from the viewpoint of a record label or an artist or band! Do you understand the benefits of this new business model? I know I do and I am already starting to implement this new business model. I have every confidence that it will work very well.

We can also start to license promo copies of our music to Third Party DJ's as another source of income. At the moment, other companies charge DJ's to play our music in public performances. Third parties are people or companies who are not considered as part of your inner circle or part of your team to put it simply. Instead of organisations such as the PRS For Music licensing DJ's to play our music releases by making them buy a DJ license direct from them, third party DJ's can pay a DJ license fee direct to the producers of any music releases i.e. Artists and bands. In order to receive advance promo copies of releases on Vinyl dubplates and acetates and on CD formats ahead of actual official release dates, DJ's can pay artists and bands direct and order a license and receive music releases exclusively before the general public can purchase copies. This is a win-win sales strategy for all musicians. Why did we never think of this before? License fees will go to the right people i.e. The creators of the music as opposed to third parties such as the PRS For Music.

With the pre-order only business model, the power is with the musicians. The pre-order business model is the perfect solution to all of our problems. The fans get to keep copies of our music and get to keep it on physical mediums which they can hold in their hands and show to their families, friends and children. It keeps the costs down and there is longevity in this method. We also take the power back from the music industry through this process. This is the beginning of the revolution in the music business. The music industry is corrupt to the core and cannot be trusted. This is why we need serious change. It has been overdue. The music industry has been ripping off artists and bands for a long time. There is no music industry without the musicians. We are the foundations of the music industry. We are the ones who make the music, record it and perform it. Without us, the music industry would not exist at all. Always remember that! We deserve some respect. After all, it is the 21st century. The future will be a lot more brighter as a result for all creative people.

Licensed DJ's who pre-order copies of DJ promo copies can play and promote our music releases for approximately 2-3 months (or in some cases much longer) prior to their official release date to the general public. During this time, any music releases can be made available to the general public to buy via pre-order only as well from online music portals, supermarkets and independent record stores etc. This way we know exactly how many copies to press up and duplicate and on what formats to make the music available on to them for purchase. Yet again, it's another win-win sales strategy for the musicians. The DJ's and fans win too.

I would also suggest that you place adverts in online and offline magazines and newspapers with links to online music portals where fans can pre-order music releases during the promotional period. You will be able to generate sales leads by advertising your music releases in the press and create more awareness for your music. You can also achieve airplay on the radio as per normal, both online and offline and get music portals listed on all the main search engines such as Google, Bing and Yahoo, so music fans can search for a music release and pre-order it instantly from officially recognized outlets. This is the way to go about creating demand for your music releases. The only real difference is that instead of pressing up copies for the sake of it, we learn how many copies to press up by taking pre-orders only. This is the future of the music business. We have to change with the times and adapt and create a sustainable business.

Fans can also pre-order music releases at gigs by either filling in a form and making payment at a music venue or by taking pre-order forms home with them and then completing them and sending payment to a specified address or by going online and making a pre-order from an online shop (Music Portal). This is the best solution for us all. This is the way to sell your music in the 21st century. It will take fans some time getting used to this new business model but they will be able to preview music releases through listening to audio clips on the internet and by watching short music videos on YouTube, for example, before actually deciding whether to make a pre-order or not. Consumer behaviour will need to change for this new sales strategy to work and it will take some time for fans to adjust to this new approach. But keep the faith. Give it time and be patient. It will work. I am convinced that this is the best way forward.

The pre-order only business model is the best way to go about things these days. Consumer behaviour needs to change in the 21st century, there's no doubt about that. The old mentality of obtaining instant copies and instant downloads of your music has to alter. It is much more preferable to take pre-orders for your music releases so you know exactly how many copies to press up on CD, Vinyl, Cassette or WAV format and let fans know that it takes up to 28 working days to ship an order to them once they have made an order as part of the pre-order terms and conditions on the website. This new business model will ensure you never press up any more copies of your music than necessary. It will also avoid having any surplus copies of your music left over which you can't get rid of. There is no point in pressing up more copies of your music releases than you need to. Pre-ordering music releases is the way forward in the 21st century. This strategy prevents colossal waste.

You can also release and sell your music on new physical mediums such as WAV format on branded USB Flash Drives. I believe this new format is a much more superior audio format and will supersede the old digital formats such as mp3 and streaming. For a start 24 Bit and 32 Bit WAV format is much better audio quality than mp3's. You should consider just selling 16 Bit and 24 Bit WAV files to the general public and retain 32 Bit WAV files as the master copies of your music and use them only for special licensing deals to compilations and for inclusion on adverts and soundtracks to films etc. In other words, only sell the master copies of your music to other businesses (B2B (Business-to-Business)) and apply the appropriate fees which can be anywhere from a few thousand pounds to a few hundred thousand pounds or more.

It would also be a wise idea to include an "end user" licensing agreement in PDF format as part of any WAV format packages on USB Flash Drives. This will ensure that "end users" are licensed to listen to your music on WAV format and it will make all the terms and conditions of the licensing agreement clear to them. Here at Uplifted Music, we currently provide licensing agreements as part of the package with sales of our music releases in WAV format on USB Flash Drives. If you need any help with this, we can help you. Please visit www.upliftedmusic.co.uk and get in touch with us. We will be happy to help.

Licensing agreements will also help to deter piracy and illegal file sharing and copying as "end users" can be prosecuted if they do not adhere to the terms and conditions of the licensing agreements as it will be a breach of contract. You can also include mp3 (320 kbit/s), WMA and whichever other digital formats which are current and relevant and which you wish to use as part of your music releases as additional files with the packages on USB Flash Drives. You can also charge a lot more for this new physical medium. You will require separate licensing agreements for each type of customer, for example – the general public and corporations. So, you can do both B2C (Business-to-Consumer) sales which is regarded as the general public and B2B (Business-to-Business) sales which is regarded as corporations.

Fans will be able to play your music in their cars by plugging in their USB Flash Drives with your music on them in WAV format and other devices. They can make a copy of your music on to their desktop computers, laptops, tablets and mobile phones. The USB Flash Drive packages can also include artwork and information relating to your music such as songwriting, sound engineering and producer credits. As with pre-orders for CD's and vinyl, you can also take pre-orders for WAV format on USB Flash Drives, so you know exactly how many copies to make. Yet again, this is another win-win situation.

Sending promo copies of your music

Artists and bands should use mp3's as a promotional tool and send low quality mp3's (128kbit/s) only to online and offline magazines and newspapers for reviews. It may be wise to do the same with copies of your music sent to the majority of radio stations both online and offline for airplay. Don't give them high quality copies or masters of your music. This strategy will help reduce piracy and illegal file sharing and encourage people to buy high quality versions of your music direct from you on pre-order only. It will do no harm to distribute low quality versions of your music.

The old traditional method of sending out hundreds or more copies of artists and band's music on white label vinyl promos to Third Party Club DJ's (especially in the dance music scene) doesn't work in my opinion. It ends up costing you a lot of time and expense for very little in return. Club DJ's don't always complete DJ Reaction sheets and return them to the sender. They don't always let you know if they've been playing your music or not and at which venues. This form of promotion no longer is effective and is extremely counter-productive. The Club DJ's make money from paid gigs whilst we provide them with free music which is a tool for their jobs.

It simply is not worthwhile to engage in this type of promotional activity anymore. I know from personal experience. I spent somewhere in the region of a thousand pounds just sending out about a hundred promo copies to ungrateful and spoilt Club DJ's when I released my Vitality "Chemistry/Blinded By The Sun (Ode To BT)" track on 12" white label vinyl promo back in 2004/2005. The majority of Club DJ's never even acknowledged receiving copies of my record or said "thanks". A "thank you" would have been very nice or "thanks for sending me this promo, but I am not interested in this type of music, so please don't send any more promos to me" or something on those lines! This was a wasted exercise and I learnt a major lesson from it. It is better to have your own inner circle of Club DJ's who are part of your street team and who will be happy to help and support you and who are licensed to play your music in public performances. You need a team of people who you can trust and who work very well together and are reliable.

Keep everything in-house as I have said before. Don't waste time and money on Club DJ's who are only interested in promoting their friend's music and receiving free music from musicians and record labels. It will only end up bankrupting you. It really is not worthwhile to continue doing this. The best approach is to release one-off Vinyl Dubplates and Acetates on your own Music Portal about three months prior to an official pre-order release date for your single or album to the general public. These can be made available to Third Party Club DJ's to pre-order directly from your own Online Shop and you can provide them with a DJ license to play your music in public performances.

You can charge Third Party Club DJ's a lot more for one-off Vinyl Dubplates and Acetates and include a DJ License in the fee which will enable them to use your music in public performances. This business model will authorize them to use your music without any repercussions. It's the best solution I can think of with regard to licensing third party DJ's. Some DJ's may not be happy with these changes but if we carry on with the current business model, then only the DJ's stand to benefit from this and it will bankrupt record labels and musicians will not get compensated for DJ's using their music at paid gigs which is a vital tool for their job.

I would also advise that you upload audio clips/samples and short videos of your music to sites like YouTube to help promote a new single or album release. For example, use a thirty second or one minute clip featuring the best part of a track and produce a short video for it to keep viewers and listeners interested. You can also post these promotional videos on Facebook, Instagram and Twitter etc. The audio clips are basically an advert for your single or album release.

This is how you market and sell your music

So, let's start by going through the whole marketing and sales process one more time to make it all clear to you and to give you the basic concept of how the new business model will work in theory. Let's say as an example that you have completed the recording of your album and are ready to start releasing a few singles off your album to start promoting it. You've chosen the best songs on your album and have decided which ones to release and in what order. We will use the same strategy for each single taken from your album and also for the album release itself.

It would be a wise idea to leave a 2-6 month gap (the amount of time is entirely up to you) before distributing any copies of your music to anyone. This will give artists and bands time to promote their own music first for a while and perform live. This will also be a part of your marketing calendar which you produce for your marketing plan. So, artists themselves promote their own music for a short period of time before sending out promo copies of their music exclusively to a small circle of affiliates such as DJ's who form part of their in-house street team.

You then proceed to send out promotional copies of your music to a number of DJ's on radio stations both locally, nationally and internationally and send out low quality versions of your music only in mp3 format to them and to online and offline music magazines and newspapers for review. After a while, you start selling non-exclusive copies of your music on dubplates/acetates to third party Professional DJ's and vinyl record collectors who purchase special DJ licenses direct from your retail outlet/s such as your own Music Portal or affiliated Music Portals, again at a premium price, so that third party Professional DJ's can play and promote your music in public performances.

At the same time, you release music videos of your music releases and send these to local, national and international music channels on TV. You also release short audio/video clips of your music releases to help promote them by uploading them to YouTube and social media accounts etc. In the meantime, it is then recommended that you try to sell your music (B2B) by licensing it to others businesses such as music compilations and for use in soundtracks on films and on computer games such as Xbox and PlayStation consoles. Just send out low quality versions of your music releases in mp3 format for promotional use to obtain licensing deals with corporations. If any companies decide to license your music from you, you can then send them master copies of your music but at a premium price. Only send the master copies when they've signed and dated the licensing deals and paid you an advance fee to exploit your music.

As soon as you've completed all the promotional side of the sales business model, you can then release your music officially to the general public (B2C) and make it available for general sale. By this time, you will hopefully have created enough demand to take pre-orders of your music releases from your fans and semi-pro and amateur DJ's. By this time, you can also release your music as ringtones for mobile/cell phones. The time-scale you wish to use to implement this marketing and sales strategy is completely up to you.

I would also suggest that you start to license your music releases for use in playlists in supermarkets, gyms and on playlists for on-hold queues for customer service departments of corporations when customers are waiting to speak to someone on the phone as a way of increasing your revenue streams and to help promote your music even more. You can also sell merchandise as another additional revenue stream at gigs and on your online shop. Please refer to chapter 2 for a list of products which you can sell. It may also be possible to sell tickets to your gigs direct to fans as well. I will talk about this more in Chapter 6.

Below is an illustration of how to go about promoting and selling your music releases:

Sales Promotional Model based on the Pre-Order Only Business Model

for Music Releases in the 21st Century

DJ's -> Radio Stations/Music Channels -> Retail

Phase 1

- Artist/Band Self-Promotion
- In-house DJ's (Street Team)

Phase 2

- Radio Stations
- Magazines and Newspapers (For reviews)
- Third Party Professional DJ's
- YouTube Clips
- Music Videos on Music Channels on TV

- License Music to Compilations

- License Music to Films

- TV Adverts

- Computer Games

Phase 3

- Commercial release through Licensed Retailers

- Ringtones

- Playlists

It is essential to stagger the release of your music by doing it in phases starting with Phase 1 right through to Phase 3. I would also recommend you leave at least a three month minimum period between promotional activities to commercial pre-order release to give your music enough time to gain exposure and to create enough demand and for fans to want to go out and buy your music from licensed retailers. Similar to how music is promoted and sold now.

I'm not sure I would bother with making music releases available to download in digital formats and available to stream from services like ITunes, Apple Music and Spotify. I would only recommended selling physical formats of your music to fans. But it's entirely up to you. You could also include downloads and streaming. It's your choice at the end of the day. It just doesn't add any value to the music in my opinion and there is very little income from streaming unless you're getting millions of plays or you have a Digital Music Content licensing deal with these services. You could use streaming and mp3 downloads as an additional promotional tool. I'll leave that choice to you!

Below is a list of all the various formats you can use for promotional activities and commercial release:

Promotional Formats

- Mp3 (128 kbit/s)

- Streaming

Official Formats

- CD
- Vinyl
- Dubplates/Acetates (DJ Promo Copies Only)
- WAV
- Cassette Tape
- Mp3 (320 kbit/s)
- WMA

So, this is how you sell your music in the 21st century. I hope it all makes sense to you and you are clear on what to do and what not to do. If you require any help with selling your music on Uplifted Music, we will be able to help you and take pre-orders for your music releases or stock your music releases on a sale or return basis. In the next chapter, I will discuss the various ways which you can use to get funding for your music projects and make the dream a reality. I explain how you can go from making and recording records, getting them pressed up, distributing them and how to put on tours and do gigs around the world and how to realize your dreams. It's not as difficult as you think!

4

HOW TO GET FUNDING

In this chapter, I discuss ways in which you can kick start your music career and get funding for your music projects in the 21st century if you're currently in no position to finance it yourself. If you find yourself in circumstances where you don't have any savings, you're not rich to begin with or you haven't won the lottery recently and you're at the end of your tether and don't know which way to turn, then you may want to consider some of the following options which I've listed in this chapter. There are a number of ways you can go about raising the funds to help launch your music career and music projects and realize your dreams. I have listed most of them that I can think of in this chapter.

The music industry is currently going through a major transitional period and I don't think anyone in the music business really knows what they're doing too be honest with you and they don't seem to know how to go about funding music ventures and how to get sales of music releases anymore. I believe we need to go back to the tried and testing ways of funding music ventures and releasing music on formats that previously worked fine in the past. There has been a lot of scaremongering over the years and too many people have tried to manipulate people within the music business into abandoning the traditional ways of raising funds and releasing music. For example, streaming services seem to have taken over the retail side of the business with regards to releasing music and crowdfunding seems to have taken over the fundraising side of things instead of raising capital by issuing private or public shares in business ventures. There is no real incentive for investors through utilizing crowdfunding platforms and consumers never get to own a piece of music. Instead, they are encouraged to rent music. None of this makes good business sense to me!

According to a recent Music Week publication, CD and digital sales are on the decline. But fear not, vinyl sales have reached a 28 year high and are improving year on year according to research and the latest figures. The old reliable format which us old timers love and have a sentimental connection with really is making a comeback! Every independent record store which I walk into is stocking more and more vinyl records and all the major retailers such as HMV and the supermarket chains such as Sainsbury's are stocking vinyl releases too. Things can only keep getting better. We can no longer ignore this major development in the music business. I personally believe this is great news for all of us and a positive sign for all of us musicians out there and I also think CD sales will also improve again. I also envisage the development of WAV format released on USB Flash Drives in the future too and this new format becoming more popular with fans! So, digital sales will improve again and sales of music will keep increasing. Don't abandon ship just yet.

This chapter focuses on the financial side of the music business and explains how to go about raising the vital funds which are necessary to get things off the ground. Marketers are having to seek new and innovative ways to market and sell their music and find alternative ways to raise funds to manufacture music releases and put events on. From album launch parties to album launch screenings, people are trying everything in order to bridge the gap. You really do have to get as creative as possible in the 21st century to raise funds and market and sell your music. It's becoming a necessity. It's imperative. If you don't adapt to the current challenge which we all face, then chances are you will be left behind. As a result of all of this information which has come to light, we now need to consider as many ways as possible to fund music projects and not discount anything. You should consider the traditional ways of acquiring funds first and foremost and also the new methods if you don't have any success with the standard resources.

Make no mistake about it. The music industry is a business. Those who say it isn't are either lying to you or they are delusional. When you become an artist or form a band and start making music and selling it, you become a business if you are doing it on a professional level. So, you need to start thinking like a business does. I suggest you start to take things more seriously and act like a business. You have to take all finances into consideration and account for every single penny that you spend on your business activities. Do things legally and professionally, especially if you want to be taken more seriously in the music industry. You will get a lot more respect as a result of taking such actions. So, don't let anyone dissuade you from considering all the options at your disposal. Hire a manager that is trustworthy to take care of the business side of things if you must.

Most musicians, artists and bands usually need a record deal when they're first starting out because they don't have the funds for certain equipment or to record their music in a professional recording studio. So, with this in mind, you need to find a way of raising funds to get your music project off the ground and finance the initial stage of the project which is recording your music in a studio if you don't already have a recording or publishing deal. To do this, you will need to start a new business and open a business bank account. It may be a new record label/company or management company which you decide to start in order to run your business. It's entirely up to you!

You could start your own music business using the legal entities such as 'sole trader' or 'partnership' and open a business bank account and go official or better still, you could aim for the stars by forming your own Private Limited Company or Public Limited Company and issue shares in your business. I would not advise you to dive in head first. You will need help running a successful company. It can't be done alone. It takes a team effort. You will require people with qualifications in certain subjects, accountants and lawyers etc. It's a big undertaking but don't let that put you off! No one said it was going to be easy but give it a try. Work with people who know how to run a successful business and who know what they're doing. You don't need to do it all on your own. Don't take on too many responsibilities. Work as a team. Share the workload and assign different roles to members of your team.

If you're struggling to buy all the music equipment you need such as a guitar or drum kit to practice on and rehearse, write new material and to finance the recording of an album project in a professional recording studio, and you need help with marketing your music and putting on gigs, then this is the chapter for you. I provide you with a comprehensive account of what options are available to you and how to go about starting them. If you're going to run your own business, you will require great leadership and business management skills and plenty of previous experience. You will most likely need to assemble a team of people together to help you run your business. You will need to know what to do and what not to do and to be able to start the right type of legal business entity which you feel is the most appropriate and which you feel most comfortable and confident with and that suits your needs and requirements.

Before you consider any of the types of funding that I've listed in this chapter, you ought to consider renting equipment or studio time to record and produce music. This will prove cheaper in the long term and you will save yourself a lot of money by doing it this way. You don't necessarily need to buy music equipment outright. You could just rent it for the time that you use it for and need it. Alternatively, you could try loaning equipment such as microphones, guitars, keyboards, speakers and other vital pieces of gear which you require to record and produce your music. There is no harm in asking friends or businesses if you can borrow equipment. You've nothing to lose by asking. You could also ask businesses to sponsor you and supply the equipment which you need. If all else fails, then I would recommend you consider some of the following options which I've listed below, if not all of them.

Start a Limited Company (Ltd)

The first thing I'd suggest to you would be to start a Ltd Company if you are based in the UK or the equivalent in any country which you reside in. You can form a Ltd Company and register a new company with Companies House in the UK – www.companieshouse.gov.uk or you can use an agent. There are many agents on the internet which you can start a Limited Company formation with. Just google "Company Formation" for a list of agents and then choose the best one for you.

A Limited Company is a legal entity in its own right. It is a type of business structure which is incorporated at Companies House. It is completely separate from its owners and it can enter into contracts in its own name and is responsible for its own actions, finances and liabilities. The owners of a company are protected by 'limited liability', which means that they are only responsible for business debts up to the value of their investments or what they guarantee to the company. The company can also keep any of the profits it makes after paying any tax. Profits can then be shared and distributed amongst all its shareholders.

A Limited Company must be registered at Companies House (UK registrar of companies) as 'limited by shares' or 'limited by guarantee'. Limited by shares companies are owned by one or more shareholders and managed by one or more directors. Limited by guarantee companies are owned by one or more guarantors and managed by one or more directors. The same person can be the owner and director, so you can set up a company by yourself or with other people.

Limited companies can be found in most countries, although the detailed rules governing them vary widely. It is also common for a distinction to be made between the publicly tradable companies of the *plc* type.

For example:

The "private" types of company such as the German GmbH, Portuguese Ltda., British Ltd., Polish sp. z o.o., the Czech s.r.o., the French s.a.r.l., the Italian and Romanian s.r.l., Hungarian kft. And Slovak s.r.o.

To set up a private limited company you will need to register with Companies House. This is known as 'incorporation'. You'll need:

- A suitable company name

- An address for the company

- At least one Director

- Details of the company's shares – you need at least one shareholder

- To check what your SIC code is – this identifies what your company does

You'll also need:

- shareholders to agree to create the company and the written rules (known as the 'Memorandum and Articles of Association'

- details of people with significant control (PSC) over your company, for example anyone with more than 25% shares or voting rights

Once you have all these details, you can register your company.

Company Name

You will need to think of a name for your company. For example: "New Music Limited". First you will need to check if your company name is already in use by doing a company names search on the Companies House website. If your company name is not in use, then you can use it and register it with Companies House. Your name cannot be the same as another registered company's name. If your name is too similar to another company's name you may have to change it if someone makes a complaint.

Your name must usually end in either 'Limited' or 'Ltd'. You can include the Welsh equivalents 'Cyfyngedig' and 'Cyf' instead if you registered the company in Wales.

Company Address

Your registered office address is where official communications will be sent, for example letters from Companies House.

The address must be:

- a physical address in the UK

- in the same country your company is registered in, for example a company registered in Scotland must have a registered office address in Scotland

You can use a PO Box address. You must still include a physical address and postcode.

You can use your home address or the address of the person who will manage your Corporation Tax.

Appoint Directors and a Company Secretary

Your company must have at least one director. Directors are legally responsible for running the company and making sure company accounts and reports are properly prepared. A director must be 16 years of age or over and must not be disqualified from being a director. Directors do not have to live in the UK but companies must have a UK registered office address. Directors' names are publicly available from Companies House. Directors must provide a service address (or 'correspondence' address), which will also be publicly available. If they use their home address, they can ask Companies House to remove it from the register.

Company Secretaries

You do not need a company secretary for a private limited company. Some companies use them to take on some of the director's responsibilities.

The company secretary can be a director but cannot be:

the company's auditor

an 'undischarged bankrupt' - unless they have permission from the court

The restrictions placed on a person when they're made bankrupt usually end when they're free from their debts (known as 'discharged'). You can check if someone has been discharged using the Insolvency Register. Even if you have a Company Secretary, the Director/s are legally responsible for the company.

Shares and shareholders

Most limited companies are 'limited by shares'. This means they're owned by shareholders, who have certain rights. For example, directors may need shareholders to vote and agree changes to the company. Most companies have 'ordinary' shares. This means directors get one vote on company decisions per share and receive dividend payments.

Work out your shares

A company limited by shares must have at least one shareholder, who can be a director. If you're the only shareholder, you'll own 100% of the company. There's no maximum number of shareholders.

The price of an individual share can be any value. Shareholders will need to pay for their shares in full if the company has to shut down. You can choose a low share value (for example, £1) to limit the shareholders' liability to a reasonable amount.

Issuing your initial shares

When you register a company you need to provide information about the shares (known as a statement of capital). This includes:

the number of shares of each type the company has and their total value - known as the company's 'share capital'

the names and addresses of all shareholders - known as 'subscribers' or 'members'

Example

A company that issues 500 shares at £1 each has a share capital of £500.

Prescribed particulars

You also need to include information about what rights each type of share (known as 'class') gives the shareholder. This information is known as 'prescribed particulars' and must include:

- what share of dividends they get
- whether they can exchange ('redeem') their shares for money
- whether they can vote on certain company matters
- how many votes they get

Memorandum and articles of association

When you register your company you need:

- a 'memorandum of association' - a legal statement signed by all initial shareholders agreeing to form the company
- 'articles of association' - written rules about running the company agreed by the shareholders, directors and the company secretary

Memorandum of association

You can use the memorandum of association template which can be found at the Companies House website. You cannot update the memorandum once the company has been registered.

Articles of association

You can use standard articles (known as 'model articles').

You can write your own articles but if you do, you cannot register your company online.

Community interest companies

You cannot use limited company model articles if you're setting up a Community Interest Company (CIC). You will need to use the CIC regulator's model constitutions instead.

Register your company

You can register your company if you have everything you need to set it up.

Register online

You can only register online if all of the following apply to your company:

- it is limited by shares
- it uses standard articles of association ('model articles')

It currently costs £12 to register online and can be paid by debit or credit card or by PayPal if you have an account. Your company is usually registered within 24 hours. If you choose not to use 'limited' in your company name, you must register your company by post using a form known as IN01.

You can also use this service to:

- register for Corporation Tax
- register for PAYE, to tell HMRC you're employing staff (including yourself if you're the only director)
- continue an application if you've already started registering

Register by post

You can register by post using a form known as IN01. Postal applications take 8 to 10 days and currently cost £40 (paid by cheque made out to 'Companies House').

You can be registered on the same day if you:

- get your application to Companies House by 3pm
- pay £100

Other ways to register

You can also register a Limited Company by:

- using an agent
- using third-party software

If your company is based overseas, you'll need to register as an overseas company. You can contact UK Trade and Investment (UKTI) for advice.

After you've registered

Once the company is registered you'll get a 'certificate of incorporation'. This confirms the company legally exists and shows the company number and date of formation. You'll also need to register for Corporation Tax within 3 months of starting to do business.

Register for Corporation Tax

After you've registered your company with Companies House, you'll need to register it for Corporation Tax. Most companies can register online for Corporation Tax and PAYE as an employer at the same time as registering with Companies House. You'll need to register for Corporation Tax within 3 months of starting to do business. This includes buying, selling, advertising, renting a property and employing someone. Further details about everything you need to know about forming a corporation can be found at the Companies House website.

The advantage of starting a Limited Company or a Public Limited Company is that you can attract a wide range of investors such as Venture Capital Firms who invest money in specialist companies. By forming a company you are giving other people or companies an opportunity to share in your business ventures success and at the same time raising funds to run the business. You can also own and run your own company and pay yourself a salary plus dividends which would mean that you would be better off financially in the long term.

As soon as you have registered your new company, you can then create new share capital and issue and sell shares in your company to private investors. This will help raise funds for your business venture and will enable you to fund all aspects of the day to day running of your business such as financing the recording of your album, marketing it, pressing up copies of your music on to vinyl, CD or WAV format on USB Flash Drives and putting on live tours.

Start a Public Limited Company (Plc)

The other alternative would be to form a Public Limited Company (Plc) in the UK and issue new share capital In the hundreds of thousands or millions and sell these shares to the public. It might also prove advantageous if you float a Public Limited Company on the stock exchange or equivalent such as the LSE (London Stock Exchange) or the NYSE (New York Stock Exchange) to open more doors and attract wealthy investors who would be able to help you realize your dreams and put everything into action.

A Public Limited Company (legally abbreviated to Plc) is a type of public company under the United Kingdom company law, some Commonwealth jurisdictions, and the Republic of Ireland. It is a limited liability company whose shares may be freely sold and traded to the public (although a Plc may also be privately held, often by another Plc), with a minimum share capital of £50,000 and usually with the letters PLC after its name. Similar companies in the United States are called *publicly traded companies*. Public limited companies will also have a separate legal identity.

A PLC can be either an unlisted or listed company on the stock exchanges. In the United Kingdom, a Public Limited Company usually must include the words "public limited company" or the abbreviation "PLC" or "plc" at the end and as part of the legal company name. I must also mention that it is possible to buy an off the shelf company which is ready made. An off the shelf company is a limited company which has been pre-registered at Companies House in the UK, but which has never traded, and is ready to be used immediately. All you would need to do is change the name of the company and declare that it is actively trading when you start trading.

Start a Charity

Another option would be to start a charity or charitable organization and accept donations from the public. A charity is a non-profit organization. The primary objectives of a charity are philanthropy and social well-being. You could start your own recording studio as an example and ask people to kindly give donations to your charity and work voluntary or for a salary and provide a service to the local community. This is probably not the best way to raise funds for your business venture especially if you are considering making music in a professional capacity and releasing it. But if you work in the music business and would like to provide a beneficial service to the public, then this might be worth considering.

A charity is defined as an organization set up to provide help and raise money for those in need. It is also defined as the voluntary giving of help, typically in the form of money, to those in need. Charities can't make profit but they can help advance the arts and relieve poverty. You could provide a charitable service to the local community by providing recording studio time to those in need. Charities have to state what their charitable objectives are in order to be registered with the Charity Commission, and then explain how they are meeting them in their annual reports, which are publicly available. To be a charity, it has to be of benefit to the public, whether that be in a geographic area or for people with a specific characteristic.

In the UK, unless your charity is a specific type of charity that doesn't have to register, you must apply to register your charity with the commission once it has an income of over £5,000. If your charity is a charitable incorporated organization (CIO) you must apply to register it whatever its income. You could set up a website and include buttons on your website to accept donations. PayPal provides buttons for websites but you will need to create an account with PayPal first. There are other websites such as JustGiving.com which you can incorporate into your social media to start accepting donations from the public.

Crowdfunding

There are many crowdfunding platforms available for you to choose from on the internet. Some are for a variety of types of businesses and others are more specialized for music business ventures. Crowdfunding is the practice of funding a project or venture by raising small amounts of money from a large number of people, typically via the Internet. Crowdfunding is a form of crowdsourcing and alternative finance. In 2015, a worldwide estimate totaling over US$34 billion was raised by crowdfunding.

Although similar concepts can also be executed through mail-order subscriptions, benefit events, and other methods, the term crowdfunding refers to Internet-mediated registries. This modern crowdfunding model is generally based on three types of actors: the project initiator who proposes the idea or project to be funded, individuals or groups who support the idea, and a moderating organization (the "platform") that brings the parties together to launch the idea.

Crowdfunding has been used to fund a wide range of for-profit, entrepreneurial ventures such as artistic and creative projects and community-oriented social entrepreneurship projects. I would recommend giving crowdfunding a go, especially if you are unable to raise funds for your music projects via the options I have listed above. Below is a list of some examples of crowdfunding websites for artists and bands wishing to record music and release it to the public.

- Crowdfunder.co.uk

- Pledgemusic.com

PledgeMusic is a unique marketplace where artists and fans can connect and support their favourite artists. PledgeMusic is an online direct-to-fan music platform, launched in August 2009, that facilitates musicians reaching out to their fan base to pre-sell, market, and distribute music projects including recordings, music videos, and concerts.

According to their website, Kickstarter is the world's largest funding platform for creative projects. Kickstarter which was founded in 2009 is an American public-benefit corporation based in Brooklyn, New York, that maintains a global crowdfunding platform focused on creativity and merchandising. The company's stated mission is to "help bring creative projects to life". There are many other crowdfunding platforms which you can choose from. These are just a few examples. I would suggest you use search engines such as Google and Bing to find the most appropriate crowdfunding platform for your business venture. However, please be aware that these types of crowdfunding platforms act as middlemen and you would be much better off forming a Ltd company or Plc to begin with. Use crowdfunding platforms as a last resort as they take a considerable percentage of the money you raise.

Sponsorship

Sponsorship is a form of affinity marketing that provides certain rights and benefits to the buyer or "sponsor". It is usually in conjunction with a property, venue, personality, or event. Sponsorship advertising is a form of advertising where a company will sponsor some event or organization. Companies should consider such factors as the relevance of the event or organization to its business, brand fit, any misalignment of interests, and the probable business result of a sponsorship before pursuing it. If you decide to take the sponsorship route, then this might be one of the best ways forward for you to raise funds for your business or music venture. You would need to consider approaching as many businesses as possible for sponsorship opportunities. Sponsorship is one of the fastest growing forms of marketing. It can be a very powerful key to a business's marketing plan. You could start by approaching local businesses or major brands. For example, one of the music compilations which my music was featured on in Taiwan was sponsored by Coors Light, the brewing company based in the USA.

Endorsements

Endorsements are a form of advertising that uses famous personalities or celebrities who command a high degree of recognition, trust, respect or awareness amongst the people. Such people advertise for a product, lending their names or images to promote a product or service. Advertisers and clients hope such approval, or endorsement by a celebrity, will influence buyers favourably. Endorsements are probably a last resort if all other options for funding are ruled out. It might not be an option for some artists and bands in the early stages of their music career, but if they are well-established, then this is an option which you might want to consider. You could also consider asking an established artist or band or celebrity to endorse your music project or music releases.

Business Loan

A business loan is a loan specifically intended for business purposes. As with all loans, it involves the creation of a debt, which will be repaid with added interest. There are a number of different types of business loans, including bank loans, mezzanine financing, asset-based financing, invoice financing, microloans, business cash advances and cash flow loans

Obviously, the last thing you want to do is get into debt in order to fund your music venture. But as a last resort, borrowing money might be the only option for you in order to get your music project off the ground. A business loan will be a cheaper form of a loan compared to a personal loan. You would need to approach a bank and open a business account and assess which business loans are available to you. I would recommend you choose a business loan with the lowest interest rates.

Personal Loan

A personal loan is money borrowed from a bank, credit union or online lender that you pay back in fixed monthly payments, typically over two to five years. Most personal loans are "unsecured" — not backed by collateral. Again, this would be a last resort in order to finance your music venture and could be deemed very risky. I would recommend that you choose a personal loan with the lowest interest rate.

Credit

Credit is the ability of a customer to obtain goods or services before payment, based on the trust that payment will be made in the future. It is possible to get credit in the form of credit cards. In the past, when I released my first album on CD on my first record label – TSYT RECORDINGS in 2004, I used a combination of credit cards, personal loans and overdraft facilities to finance the recording and release of my first album. However, this is not a good way to finance your music venture and is very risky. Again, I would recommend that you choose credit card service providers with the lowest interest rates in order to reduce your monthly repayments and to avoid bankruptcy.

Overdraft Facility

An overdraft facility is a form of an emergency loan and allows you to write cheques or withdraw cash from your current account or business account up to the overdraft limit which is approved by your bank. It is a short-term (usually up to 12 months) standby credit facility which is usually renewable on a yearly basis. It is repayable on demand by the bank at any time. I would recommend using an overdraft facility as opposed to taking out credit or borrowing money in the form of a personal or business loan. Again, you want to avoid getting into debt and you would need to find the best deal out there by researching all the costs and interest charges which banks expect from you in return for providing such a service.

Pre-Order Business Model

The Pre-Order business model is fast becoming one of the most preferred ways of raising the funds required to release music. If you are planning on releasing your music on physical formats such as CD or vinyl or a combination of both, then I would highly recommend that you choose this option. A Pre-Order business model is based on a business that sells items to customers on pre-order, then makes an order with a manufacturer, then distributes the product to customers. It is possible to take advance orders for your product (music releases) ahead of scheduled release dates. This involves very little financial risk and there is less chance of you ending up in debt and having to file for bankruptcy. This is a win-win situation for artists who need to raise the funds to release their music on physical formats. I believe it will become standard practice for many businesses in the 21st century.

Save up

This is quite an obvious option, but it might be your safest bet. Saving up the money to fund your music venture is less risky and less stressful. However, it may take you a long time, perhaps years and years to save up enough money to buy music equipment, pay for recording studio time and to press up your music on various formats such as vinyl or CD. There Is less chance of you ending up in debt and having to file for bankruptcy this way.

Work several jobs

For an artist, this is probably the last thing you want to hear and most likely, the last option you would want to consider. However, it may be your only way of raising the funds to realize your music project. The advantage would be that you avoid getting into debt. The disadvantage would be that you would have very little time to make and record music and you would end up very tired and exhausted. This may be a last resort and your only feasible option.

Business Partners

As one option, you could partner up with other people or other companies and work together in order to get your music projects off the ground. The term 'business partner' can have a wide range of meanings, with one of the most frequent being a person who, along with another person, plays a significant role in owning, managing, or creating a company (two best friends who start a business together would consider themselves business partners). A business partner is a commercial entity with which another commercial entity has some form of alliance. This relationship may be a contractual, exclusive bond in which both entities commit not to ally with third parties. Business partners can pitch together and invest funds in a music project on an equal basis. Sharing the costs of a music project is less risky and a good way of raising the finance needed to get your project off the ground.

I hope this chapter has provided you with some handy tips and has been very useful for you and I hope it has provided you with some more ideas about how to get funding for your music venture or ventures which you may not have already considered. In the next chapter, I discuss other sources of income which you can use to help supplement your income from music related products and sustain your music career in the 21st century.

5

OTHER SOURCES OF INCOME

In this chapter, I discuss relevant ways in which you can capitalize on additional revenue streams and other sources of income in the 21st century to make your music projects a reality. I have listed as many ways as I could in this chapter that I could think of at this present time. You have a few options available to you. You could start off by running your own business and looking for deals with other companies and deal directly with them or you could look at signing a record deal and music publishing deal and then letting them look after your business affairs and license your music to third parties. Whichever way you choose to go about it, keep persevering and never give up. Most of the time it comes down to luck. Sometimes it's being in the right place at the right time and meeting the right contacts. Either way, you have to do a lot of networking with people in order to establish the right connections and be successful in the business world.

Do you have the business acumen to be a success on your own? Or would you prefer to concentrate on making music and performing at gigs and let someone else deal with the business side of things? It's completely up to you of course. Whatever you feel is the best way to approach the music business, then go with your gut instincts. Just bear in mind, that some artists get signed to major record labels and think they've made it big time and are going to be a huge success but then get left out in the cold and on the substitutes bench, so to speak and never get to perform again. Some record labels will sign as many acts as possible and give them a deal, but will only focus on one of those artists and support and back them more than the other artists they've signed. Sometimes labels do this to stifle competition from other artists and record labels. Just when you think you are about to become a big success, you can end up being left out in the cold and never recover from it.

Be aware of some record companies. They don't always have your best interests at heart. It may prove complicated getting out of a record deal which you have signed and could be very costly. You may end up having to get a lawyer and go through the courts to get released from any contractual obligations. If you sign a record deal with the wrong company, it may be difficult to release new music under your artist or band name. Prince and George Michael had issues with the record labels they were signed to in the past and Prince had to change his artist name in order to get around the problem. Prince (who died in 2016) was an American singer, songwriter, musician, record producer and filmmaker. He had to change his artist name several times and used other names such as "The Artist Formerly Known As Prince (TAFKAP)" and "($\male$)" (also known as the "Love Symbol")".

In 1993, Prince had a contractual dispute with the record label he was signed to at the time which was Warner Bros. He changed his name to an unpronounceable symbol and began releasing new albums at a faster rate to remove himself from any obligations to the label. It wasn't until 2000, that he began to refer to himself again as "Prince" when he was signed to Arista Records. During a lawsuit in 1993 with Warner Bros, Prince appeared in public with the word "slave" written on his cheek. He was involved in a legal battle over the artistic and financial control of his musical output. Both Prince and George Michael are dead now and both died relatively young which I find somewhat suspicious. George Michael also died in 2016 and at the time of his death, he had sold over 115 million records worldwide.

George Michael was involved in a lawsuit with Sony, the record company he was signed to at the time in 1991. He believed that Sony had not completely supported the release of his second album which resulted in its poor performance in the United States compared to his previous album release. He appeared in a music video for his single release "Fast Love" in April 1996 on a chair with all speakers on it. One of the dancers in this music video appeared in a scene with a pair of headphones on with "FONY" written on the side of them which took a swipe at the record company he was previously signed to – SONY. These are just a few examples of the problems which some recording artists have with the record companies they are signed to. This is just the tip of the iceberg. Sometimes, the only way to get out of a record deal is to use a different artist name and release new music on another label.

I am telling you all this information so that you know what to expect and so that you know how to overcome any hurdles that are in your way should the situation arise. You never know what to expect when signing a record deal. It could be the start of something fantastic or it could become a complete nightmare. This is why you should consider all the options available to you first and make a wise choice when it comes to your career in the music business. Try to avoid selling your soul to the devil. I am not suggesting that you too will have problems when signing a record deal, or that all record companies are bad. I am simply illustrating some of the issues that artists have when signed to record companies. Even the major recording artists have stumbling blocks. Not everything is always plain sailing!

I hope you understand what you are letting yourself in for when signing a record deal. It can be heaven or hell. It's a complete lottery. Sometimes it can be the best decision you'll ever make in your lifetime, whereas other times it might be the worst decision you could ever make. When it comes to the money side of the business, artists and record labels always have a habit of falling out and things can turn quite nasty. This chapter will help you to decide which path to take with your music career and which option will suit you the best. If you choose to start your own record label and music publishing company, then it will mean you have to do all the hard work yourself to license your music to other companies. But you will be free from contractual obligations and you will be able to use your artist name on any music you release and will always be able to release new music without any setbacks. If it's the Do-it-yourself route which you take, then good luck to you! You get a lot of respect from me if you do decide to take that path.

There is no money in streaming music

It may be difficult to make money from digital sales of your music at the moment but there are other revenue streams that you can use to generate an income from your music. It would be foolish to rely solely on income from streaming platforms and digital downloads if you decide to release your music yourself and distribute it to all the streaming services such as Spotify and download sites such as ITunes. Artists do not receive much in terms of income from streaming platforms unless they have a licensing deal in place with them. I would only recommend uploading your music to digital music content platforms such as Spotify as a promotional tool and I would not expect to receive much at all in the way of royalties.

I know of a dance music (trance) artist called "The Thrillseekers" who had hit records in the past with some of his releases such as "Synaesthesia" in 1999 which was a critically acclaimed track and he has had over a million streams on Spotify, but yet received just £30 in royalties. This is outrageous! Spotify is essentially an online digital music jukebox. In a pub in the United Kingdom for example, a customer would pay £1 for 3 plays on a digital music jukebox which is the equivalent of 3 streams on Spotify. Playing a track on a jukebox is no different to streaming a track on Spotify. There is no real difference. The word "streaming" is just technical jargon designed to confuse the music industry and the public. Streaming platforms are a complete joke and waste of time in my opinion and serve no real purpose other than promoting an artist or band and their music. The only people that really stand to gain from streaming platforms are the employees at Spotify, the directors and the shareholders.

So, if I were you I'd rule out making your music available on sites such as Spotify unless you want to utilize it as a cheap promotional tool. It's not worth having your music on there. The only way you would stand to gain financially from it, would be by having a licensing deal with them prior to releasing your music on there, which would mean that Spotify would have to pay you a digital music content licensing fee on a monthly or quarterly basis regardless of how many streams your music was getting. This is the only way to make it profitable. You have to be very business minded when dealing with these type of companies who are just exploiting music content on their platforms for their own personal gain at the expense of the artists. I have had a couple of releases on Spotify which have generated thousands of streams worldwide but I have never been paid a penny for any of them. I very much doubt I will ever let them use my music content ever again.

Vinyl is making a comeback

Sales of music have been falling in the last two decades. However, sales of vinyl records are starting to increase year on year and the vinyl format is starting to make a major comeback as fans start to realize that mp3 and streaming formats don't offer the same value and audio quality as vinyl, CD's and WAV format. Digital downloads and streaming formats have been performing well over the last decade, but sales of CD's are still very high. I recommend that you release your music on all the available formats and any new formats that appear in the future if you want to be truly successful in the music business. Try catering to all your fan's needs. Give them the choice. Let them decide how they want to listen to your music and how they want to buy it. Let them decide if they want to rent it and pay a subscription fee to Spotify or own a copy of your music on vinyl or CD etc.

At the end of the day, you want to gain as much exposure for your music as possible. So, releasing your music on every single format is the best way forward. But don't rely on income from streaming platforms alone like some artists do. You should take all this into account and utilize other sources of income through licensing deals etc. I recommend that you consider all avenues and use all the revenue streams which are available to you if you want to fund your music projects and have a long term career in the industry and survive the music business in this century. It will do you no harm whatsoever to contemplate every single revenue stream that you can in order to be successful. If you're releasing your own music on your own record label and looking for licensing deals through your own music publishing company, then make no mistake, it's going to be hard work but it will be worthwhile in the end! Just think of the satisfaction you'll get from clinching all the deals.

Sign a record deal

A record label, or record company, is a brand or trademark associated with the marketing of music recordings and music videos. Sometimes, a record label is also a music publishing company that manages such brands and trademarks, coordinates the production, manufacture, distribution, marketing, promotion and enforcement of copyright for sound recordings and music videos. It also conducts talent scouting and the development of new artists and maintains contracts with recording artists and their managers. The term "record label" derives from the circular label in the center of a vinyl record which prominently displays the manufacturer's name, along with other information.

Recording artists have traditionally been reliant upon record labels to broaden their consumer base, market their albums, and be both promoted and heard on music streaming services, radio and television. However, an increasing number of artists have sought to avoid costs and gain new audiences via the internet, often with the help of music videos. Combined with the decline in album sales and rapid growth in free content available online, this has changed the way the industry works dramatically since the beginning of the 21st century. It has caused record labels to seek new sources of profit, in particular via "360" deals. These new types of deals which are being made with artists are called "multiple rights" or "360" deals. They give the record labels rights and percentages to artist's touring, merchandising and endorsements. In exchange for these rights, labels usually give higher advance payments to artists.

The traditional way of entering the music business has always been to sign a record deal with a record label. The usual method is to approach as many record labels as possible who would fit your style of music and try and obtain a record deal with them. This is the usual way to get help to fund the recording and manufacturing of an album. I would strongly advise you to get a manager first who can represent you as the artist or band. I would also recommend that you get yourself a music lawyer too. The majority of record companies do not accept unsolicited demos and tend to deal with managers when it comes to business affairs. It's also advantageous to have a lawyer who can read through all the contracts you have to sign with the various companies.

You will need to make contact with someone in the A&R department at the record company and let them know to expect your music in the post or better still, arrange a meeting with them at their office with your manager, so they can listen to your music at an agreed appointment face-to-face. There is more chance of the record label listening to your music and signing you if you meet them face-to-face or if they come to watch you play live. Otherwise, chances are your music will be thrown in the bin and will never get listened to due to the amount of unsolicited demos which the record labels receive on a daily basis. Some record labels receive hundreds of demos every day. So, as you can imagine it is very difficult to get a major record deal and grab their attention. Your music is like a needle in a haystack. You have to be different.

Your music Is more likely to get listened to if you send it to a small record label that doesn't receive many demos in the post. You're more likely to get a response from a smaller label than a big label and there is less chance of your music being ignored and thrown in the bin. You are also more likely to receive feedback from them which is always very useful. The only downside is that they probably won't be able to afford to pay you as much money as a major record company would and will not have as big a marketing budget and your music would not receive as much exposure to begin with. The positive aspect would be that signing to a small record label would give you a platform to break into the industry and get recognized and develop your music and it's always possible that your music could be licensed to a bigger record company sometime in the future. It is best to take whatever opportunities come your way!

It also helps if you have a solid fan base to begin with which can be developed and expanded upon. Especially in the local area where you are based. Any record label looking to sign artists wants someone who they can market and sell your music to. If you have a strong following on social media and lots of fans turn up to every gig you play, then there is more chance of you signing a record deal. It's important to do some of the groundwork yourself to increase your chances of getting a deal. Don't just rely on family and friends to support you. You will need a real fan base. Record labels aren't stupid. They know which artists and bands have a real solid fan base. There will be a buzz about your music and your live performances and word will spread. If your music is very original, unique and of high quality, then you should have no problems acquiring a recording contract whatsoever.

Sign a music publishing deal

In the music industry, a music publisher (or music publishing company) is responsible for ensuring the songwriters and composers receive payment when their music compositions are used commercially. They also secure commissions for music and promote existing compositions to recording artists, films and television. Through an agreement called a "music publishing contract", a songwriter or composer assigns the copyright of their music or composition to a music publishing company. In return, the music publishing company then licenses compositions, helps monitor where compositions are used, collects royalties and distributes them to the composers. If you've not already considered signing a music publishing deal, then perhaps this is one of your best options to secure other sources of income for your music. Use the internet to search for names, addresses, websites and contact details of music publishing companies and send them your music or make an appointment to see them at their office.

It would be an idea to approach as many different music publishing companies as you can that best fit your style of music and present your music to them in a professional manner. I would recommend using the same strategy as you would with a record label. Do not send them unsolicited demos and recruit a manager to help represent you and arrange meetings with music publishing executives to get them to listen to your music in person. As I'm sure with record labels, music publishing companies most likely also receive hundreds of demos every day and are overwhelmed by the sheer number of artists looking for help. Your best bet is to meet them face-to-face and play your music to them at a scheduled appointment. This will increase your chances of signing a music publishing deal and will save you a lot of time and effort trying to get licensing deals yourself. But remember not to sign the rights of your music over to anyone unless they pay you a hefty advance prior to any licensing deals which they obtain with third parties.

Start your own Record Label or Music Publishing Company

If you find it difficult to get a record deal or music publishing deal after sending out demos to A&R departments for example, you could start your own record label or music publishing company as an alternative and approach third party companies yourself and try and license your music to them that way instead. The market is very competitive though, so you will have to try very hard to obtain licensing deals but I would advise you to keep persevering with it. Don't give up at the first hurdle. Just keep trying until you start to establish contacts and develop strong relationships with third party companies. Just bear in mind that you will be competing with thousands of other artists, record labels and music publishing companies. So, don't expect an easy ride!

To begin with, you could start your own record label and release an E.P. with say about four of your best tracks included on it and use that as a platform to get your music out there and grab the attention of bigger record labels. Starting your own business will also be useful as you will have a few options available to you for help with funding your music projects. If you open a business banking account you will be offered business loans, credit and overdraft facilities which could help you finance the manufacture, marketing and release of your music and most importantly pay yourself a wage.

If you start your own music publishing company you could also publish your own music and give yourself a music publishing deal. I did this myself in the past when I started my first record label – TSYT RECORDINGS in 2004. I formed TSYT Music Publishing Ltd in 2005 and self-published my own music as I was finding it difficult to get a music publishing deal with anyone else at the time. It helped pay for equipment and the manufacture of my first album. You could approach executives who work for TV Shows and license your music to them for use on their TV channels or television programs. You could consider supplying the music for commercials on the radio and TV, films, jingles, computer games, social media adverts and adult entertainment movies and channels etc. You could also sell your music as ringtones for mobile phone devices. There are many choices for you to consider and try. So use all the options that are available to you at the time.

If you find it quite demanding trying to license your music to well established third party companies and are not having much luck with getting any deals, I suggest you try approaching new business start-ups or small companies who will be more keen and eager to work with you. You could even partner up with a film maker and provide them with the soundtrack to their film and work out a deal where you would receive a percentage of sales from digital downloads or from copies sold of the film on DVD or Blu-Ray or from ticket sales in the cinema. There are many things you could do to improve your chances of getting paid for your music. You just have to use your initiative and improvise wherever necessary. Just don't give up!

The main sources of income

The main sources of income for you from music releases will be royalties that are generated from TV and radio airplay. You will either need a music publishing company working on your behalf to collect royalties which are due or you will need to join a royalty collecting society such as the PRS For Music. It is completely up to you how you decide to go about this. You could also collect royalties yourself by creating licensing agreements with any of the companies that use your music by starting your own music publishing company as I have mentioned earlier in this chapter. Income will also be generated from sales of your music on CD, vinyl, cassette tape, mp3's (digital downloads), WAV format on USB Flash Drives, DVD's and Blu-Rays etc.

Ringtones are a very lucrative business as well. It is an extremely profitable industry for major record labels with a revenue of over £5 billion a year worldwide. You could sell ringtones through third party ringtone portals. They take as much as 30 per cent in fees and help many independent artists, or alternatively, you could sell ringtones on your own music portal as an additional revenue stream and cut out the unnecessary middlemen. There are many other ways you can generate an income through your music by selling advertising space on your artist website or on a music portal if you own one. You can get sponsorship for your gigs, album and single releases and also sponsorship for your music videos. This would involve including any sponsors logos on your music releases to get them publicity in return for sponsoring your releases and events.

You could also get companies to sponsor your newsletters that you send out to your fan base on a mailing list which you put together. Another suggestion would be to give away free sampler CD's which feature new music releases or previously unreleased tracks or mixes to your fans and ask a company to sponsor the marketing exercise. It would benefit both the artist and the sponsor and create more awareness of your music and would help gain publicity for the company sponsoring it. Your ability to attract regular and sufficient traffic to your website or music portal would give sponsors more incentive to sponsor your products and events etc. as this would help raise their public profile.

I would propose licensing your music to music compilations and computer games such as X-Box and PlayStation console games as an additional source of income. These types of licensing deals can often be very lucrative and help promote your music even further and build a bigger fan base all over the globe. You could upload music videos to YouTube and get paid for adverts that are played before your video starts. You can also expect to create an income from sales of tickets for gigs, endorsements and merchandise sales. You'll be one of the lucky ones if you do obtain any endorsements from well-known brands and companies. So, don't rule these other sources of income out. You can sell T-Shirts, Caps, Hoodies, Posters, Live Recordings, Keyrings and Fridge Magnets and much more! You could also have multiple sponsors and explore additional sponsorship deals with other companies to help promote their products, services and brands in combination with your music releases or music videos or at events as another option.

You might also want to consider accepting donations on your website or music portal for charitable causes and help the local community and give something back to them. You could charge appearance fees for appearing on television or radio programs or at any events. This is another valuable source of income that you may not have considered before. Try not to overlook anything and give everything a go. Evaluate what works the best and stick at it. Anything that doesn't work so well, stop doing it and just focus on the revenue streams that provide you with a steady income. I'm sure there are numerous other things you could do to bring in more money to help you to sustain your music career, but I have listed most of them that I can think of in this chapter. So, that should suffice for the time being. Try to be as creative as possible and come up with original concepts and new ideas that haven't been done before so you are one step ahead of the rest.

Venture Capitalists

Another suggestion would be to use your networking skills and make contact with Venture Capitalists to seek funding for your business. You can do this by using social networking tools such as LinkedIn.com or search the internet for contacts and visit their websites. As soon as you have made contact, you can present your ideas to them and put forward a business plan to attract investment. A Venture Capitalist is an investor who either provides capital to startup ventures or supports small companies that wish to expand but which do not have access to equities markets. Venture capitalists are usually willing to invest in such companies because they can earn a massive return on their investments if these companies are successful.

Venture capitalists also experience major losses when the companies they've invested in fail, but these types of investors are typically wealthy enough that they can afford to take the risks associated with funding young, unproven companies that appear to have a great idea and a great management team. So, this might well be an avenue worth exploring if you're still struggling to fund your business venture after starting your own record label or music publishing company. I recommend that you give it a go as working with other people may benefit your music projects in the long run. Venture Capitalists may have years of experience with working with new businesses and they may also be able to contribute to your music projects with ideas and suggestions which will help your business move forward and be more successful. It will do you no harm to forge a business partnership with a wealthy investor. So, if all else fails, give it a go. You've nothing to lose!

Below is a list of all the various licensing options and other ways in which you can earn an income from your music which I have described in this chapter, whether it be directly or indirectly from sales of your music or your brand:

Licensing Deals

Music Publishing:

- TV Shows
- Commercials (Radio & TV)
- Films
- Computer Games
- Gaming Consoles (Xbox & PlayStation)
- Ringtones
- Jingles
- Social Media Ads
- YouTube Ads
- Podcasts
- Adult Entertainment Movies
- Adult Entertainment TV Channels

Sales from Merchandise on a Music Portal and at Gigs

Merchandise:

- T-Shirts
- Posters (Signed and Limited Editions)
- Hoodies
- Live Recordings (CD/Vinyl/WAV)
- Coffee Mugs
- Hats
- Keyrings
- Programs
- Fridge Magnets
- Mouse Pads/Mats

Touring:

- Ticket Sales

Royalties from Airplay

Airplay:

- TV (Dedicated Music Channels)
- TV Programs
- TV Adverts
- Radio
- Radio Adverts

Income from endorsements

Endorsements:

- Clothes (Fashion)
- Cars
- Drinks

Income from sponsorship deals

Sponsorship:

- Single releases
- Album releases
- Music Videos

- Free Sampler CD's

- Newsletters

- Artist/Band website

- Music Portal

I hope this chapter of my book has been very useful, educational and helpful to you. If you can think of any other ideas for sources of income, then you are welcome to give them a try. Do not be afraid to try out different things. All the methods I have described in this chapter are just examples for you to work with. At the end of the day, you need to eat and keep a roof over your head. So, it's imperative that you have a steady flow of income coming in to keep everything going and pay all the bills.

It is completely up to you how you go about creating additional revenue streams from your music releases and live performances. I hope you will follow some of my suggestions. Remember, the music industry is a business. If you don't have a regular income from your music, then you are very unlikely to survive in the industry. I found that out in the early stages of my music career and learnt the hard way. I don't want you to make the same mistakes as I did and go through the kind of hell I went through.

The next chapter is about Music Portals and how I believe they are the future of the music industry in the 21st century. Record labels no longer have the power they used to have. Music Portals are starting to replace the traditional record label which has dominated the music industry for many decades. I will explain how Music Portals cover all aspects of the music business from providing up to date information about artists and their music releases and tours and how they can cover the distribution and retail side of the music business too!

6

MUSIC PORTALS – THE FUTURE OF INFO, DISTRIBUTION & RETAIL

In this chapter, I discuss the future of the music industry in the 21st century and strategies to overcome modern day problems with distribution and retail. The music industry has gone through many changes and transitions over the last few decades as we have already discussed. With the rise of the internet as a major player in the distribution of online music, you'd have thought the quality of life would have improved for many musicians with the ease of access to a global market, but the reality is that things have become much more worse and it's become even more difficult for independent artists to get paid and earn a living from making music as the industry has been boxed off. This is partly due to the market being flooded with so much music and a lack of quality control when it comes to what music is available for sale at a retail level. Most musicians start their own record labels now and release their own music meaning there are even more people trying to get a share of the market. It's also as a result of streaming and cloud based music services becoming more and more popular with the younger generations of music consumers.

The younger generation of music consumers expect everything that's on the internet for free and they do not value physical formats in the same way the older generations do. This new business model has made music much more accessible to fans on a global scale, but at the same time it has devalued music and digital music platforms such as Spotify tend to only pay artists and bands with licensing agreements in place and they are usually artists that are signed to major record companies. So, independent artists and bands continue to struggle and there is even less money to go round. Not much has changed in that respect. The problem that artists face now is how to generate enough revenue to make music pay and to make it worthwhile investing time and money into music projects. You'll be glad to know, there is a solution for the independent artists and bands in the 21st century - Music Portals!

Music Portals are basically futuristic Record Companies that are more forward thinking than their predecessors. In a hundred years from now, Record Companies will have been completely replaced by Music Portals which will cover all aspects of the music business from manufacturing records, marketing artists, organizing gigs, selling and distributing their music all over the globe. These futuristic portals which can be accessed online, 24/7, all over the world will have a presence on the worldwide web and will radically transform the way we do business. They will supply us with a new way of providing information to fans at the touch of a button and will also present us with a new method for distributing and selling our music on the worldwide web and in high street shops in physical and digital formats.

This new concept gives us a way of cutting out all the greedy middlemen (to put it simply) who have dominated the music business for decades and who have always taken a big slice of the pie and who rarely or never give any slices of the pie to the original creators of the music. So, artists and bands tend to end up going hungry as a result of this. This attitude towards musicians can no longer continue. Otherwise, if artists never earn any income from making music, it will have a major knock on effect and companies making musical instruments will suffer as musicians are no longer able to afford the costs attributed with making music. Sales will decrease worldwide and music will no longer be a viable business to get involved in. The only solution we have is to take back control of the music industry and cover the retail side of the music business ourselves. Owning or co-owning your own Music Portal or being affiliated to one and selling your music direct to the fans will be a revolutionary breakthrough and it means that you will put yourself in the driving seat and back in control of the revenue streams. Make no mistake about this. It could be the solution we've all been waiting for. There is no doubt in my mind that it will revolutionize the music industry and transform things for the better.

There's little point making and selling music if you're not receiving anything back for it unless it's just a hobby to you or you are super rich to begin with. After all, you can't go on starving or not being able to pay all your bills. It's just not practical and realistic. It's a job at the end of the day. And if you're selling music then it no longer is a hobby. So, in this respect, it's very important that you receive a slice of the pie so that you can continue to do what you love doing and reinvest money back in to recording future albums and putting on tours. This is why I wrote this chapter in my book, to help explain to you how to vastly improve your chances of getting paid for your music and make things work for you. This chapter is very helpful for artists and bands who are struggling to get any of that pie by doing the distribution of their music themselves and selling it directly to the fans whilst building and maintaining a solid fan base.

Remember, when Myspace took the internet by storm and it helped raise awareness of artists and band's music? It was like a godsend for many artists as they had a visible presence for free on the internet unlike before. It was the largest social networking site in the world at the time, from 2005 to 2009. Myspace was the original Facebook. Musicians were able to showcase their music to the world and fans were able to follow them and keep up to date with new music releases and forthcoming gigs and get in contact with them. Also, consider sites like Bandcamp which was founded in 2008 and sells music direct to fans. The company is a global music community where fans discover music and directly support the artists who make it. ReverbNation is another site which springs to mind which was launched in 2006 and of which was similar to Myspace. The Music Portal concept is nothing new. It's been around for a while now but it is only just starting to take shape and people are beginning to see the benefits of it. These social networking sites were the early foundations of Music Portals. They provided us with the vision to take music into the 21st century and beyond and a glimpse into the future and what future Record Companies would look like. It demonstrated that all artists and bands needed visibility and web space so that they could showcase their music and develop a social network of fans and sell their music directly to them.

Then came along social media platforms such as Facebook which was founded in 2004 and has dominated people's daily lives ever since, Twitter in 2006 and Instagram in 2010. Since then, there has been an abundance of different types of social media platforms to give exposure to musicians and connect more with fans such as Soundcloud which was founded in 2007 and Mixcloud which was launched in 2008. Music Portals do all these things and more! Well, that's the general idea behind the concept. There is no need to upload and distribute your music to third parties anymore. Especially, when they do not pay for music content and are not actually licensed to do so. All these third parties should be licensed to exploit your music content.

The second you upload and distribute your music to third party music content sharing platforms, your music is devalued and becomes worthless as you have given away copies of your music for free. It no longer has exclusivity. It becomes very difficult to make any money from your music once you've given away your rights in return for nothing. Music Portals remove the need for third parties to share your music with the public. The only difference with Music Portals and social networking and media platforms is that you will need to invest a lot of money into advertising your Music Portal in order to stand out from the crowd. This could take a huge investment and may take a while to develop. But if you've already been using all these other social media and social networking platforms, then the chances are that your fans already know about you and your music and you can let them know where to listen to your music and where to buy it, from now on. The most important factor in all of this is that it cuts out the need for middlemen. The middlemen being the modern day Record Labels, Distributors, Retailers and social media, networking and music sharing platforms.

No one seems to know what they're doing when it comes to running the music industry. That's how I see things. At the moment, it's all trial and error! There seems to be a power shift which is taking place and which has been going on for the last two decades. More and more middlemen are trying to get a piece of the action and present musicians with new ways to get their music heard but have still not come up with a viable solution. New concepts are popping up all the time. But there is no clear direction in the way that the music industry is heading apart from streaming platforms which I don't think help all that much. It has become apparent that there are no real leaders in the music business. No one really knows what to do and how to tackle this crisis head on. We need leadership qualities and pioneers who can take the music business into the 21st century and revolutionize the way we do business. It's all about returning control of the music business to the very people who make the music in the first place and separating the professionals from the hobbyists. There is currently no transparency when it comes to finding quality music as there is so much of it available on streaming services. Where can fans go to discover quality new music and own a copy of the music? I will explain how in this chapter.

What is a Music Portal?

What is a Music Portal you may ask? Well, a Music Portal is an online shop/store and information portal combined into one. It's very much like a Record Label website and high street shop. Music Portals are an alternative to the modern day streaming platforms and they let fans own music as opposed to renting it. They retain the traditional business model of fans being able to own copies of music releases as opposed to renting the music to listen to over an internet connection or over their Wi-Fi which can often be interrupted during playback. It is also cheaper for the consumer in the long run as they will only have to pay once to buy a music release whereas with streaming platforms they have to constantly renew their subscription which means it will cost the consumer more money in the long term and they will never own it and will always be reliant on their internet connection working or not. Only the digital streaming platforms and major record companies will prosper from streaming. Music Portals put the artists back in control. As artists and bands we have to take into consideration the fans who support us and I believe it is better to let them own copies of our music and put our faith and trust in them not to copy or share our music illegally. We have to strive to have better relationships with the fans and get closer to them in the same way we connect with them on social media and have our own media representation on the internet.

Music Portals are the next generation of record labels as I've explained before. They are not Record Companies, they do not fund the recording of your music. Not to begin with anyway. You have to raise the funds yourself to begin with to subsidize any music recording projects you get involved with. You are now expected to finance the initial recording of your own music which is the way most artists and bands have done it, previously. So, there is no change there. This has always been expected of artists and has become the norm. However, Music Portals remove the need for many middlemen such as Record Labels, Distributors and Retailers who all have a habit of taking all the proceeds from the sales of records and pocketing it themselves, leaving the artists with virtually nothing. All these middlemen are third parties providing a service to musicians and deduct as much money as they can from any sales of music.

I understand that the majority of musicians do not have the kind of marketing budgets that major record companies have which are required to launch new artists. We will always need financial help to market and sell our music, but we can vastly reduce the number of middlemen involved and keep costs down as a result of selling music direct to the fans ourselves in the same way artists sell their music to fans on sites such as Bandcamp. There are ways to acquire financial assistance to market new artists and I've explained many of them in earlier chapters of this book. Major Record Companies would usually float on the stock market and attract wealthy investors and would then reinvest all the new share capital back into marketing new artists. If you are looking to sell hundreds of thousands or millions of copies of records, you are probably going to need to spend a few million marketing artists who release their music on your Music Portal. You get back what you put in. It won't be much different to running a traditional record label. The only way to market music releases on a shoestring budget would be to use viral marketing strategies but there is no guarantee of success. Usually, you have to spend a lot of money marketing new artists to get a return. Sometimes, it can take as many as three or four albums to recoup what you spend on marketing them.

Music Portals give you the ability to connect with fans in ways which haven't been done before and they give you the ability to sell music and merchandise to fans directly. You no longer need to go through numerous middlemen to accept payment for a music release. The technology is there to do it now. Only, most people who work in the music industry and run it do not want to lose control over the revenue streams. The balance of power is shifting though. They know that and so do you, now! Music Portals are the future of the music industry and many artists and bands are starting to realize this and catch on to this new and effective business model and many people see Music Portals as the answer to many of their problems. It is a much better option than streaming music and making it all cloud based. There is very little in terms of revenue for artists who just stream their music. The music industry is clinging on to power but it's only a matter of time before Music Portals become the mainstream and put the power back in the musicians hands.

You now have the ability to cover the Record Label, Distribution and Retail side of the industry. You can now sell physical and digital products direct to fans all over the world from a single website (Music Portal) or multiple websites. You should take into consideration the amount of work involved in running your own Music Portal. Running your own business and website comes with extra responsibilities, but you won't mind doing this as it means you are more likely to get paid for your work and be successful! Right? It means doing the extra work yourself to begin with or hiring other personnel to do the extra work but you increase your chances of getting paid for your music. You take control over the distribution, marketing and sales process of your business. There is more chance of you getting a slice of the pizza. Whereas in the old days you could only hope and pray that you would be able to eat with the most likely outcome being that you'd go hungry and have to take on another job just to pay the bills and put food on your table. All the middlemen have always paid themselves first and dictated how much they got paid and usually got greedy with no concern for the original creator of the product. The only way you ever got paid for your music in the past was if you were signed to a major record company and received a yearly salary.

Hence, why in the 21st century it became necessary to take the power back and regain control over your music and make sure that the right people got paid for their work. In the past, artists and bands were always far too reliant on the old traditional business model and were always last in line to get paid when it came to royalties from sales of their music and rarely, if ever got paid. That was my first-hand experience of the music business in the past anyway! This became a major problem over the decades and musicians started to get complacent and left all the business side of things to those in charge of the record labels and as a result were majorly exploited by unscrupulous businessmen and women. They told musicians to do it for the love. Do it for the love, they said! However, it became apparent that these people were hypocrites. They were not doing it purely for the love. They were doing it for the money all along. There has been a worldwide conspiracy over the last few decades to stop the majority of musicians earning an income from their music. But since the evolution of Music Portals, it now means that musicians can become independent and run the industry themselves and free themselves from the bondage of unpaid slavery in the 21st century.

Having your own Music Portal is like having your own music shop on the high street. Only, you don't have the same overheads and costs that a high street shop has with rent and insurance etc. As soon as you have a website built and an online shop setup and installed on your website to take care of the retail side of the business, the only overheads you have with your own Music Portal is web hosting fees which are usually monthly and the yearly cost of renewing the domain name and the running costs associated with running the business. This is a lot less than what you'd be paying if you were running a high street shop. A Music Portal is an online shop/store which automates a transaction and does everything automatically. You just have to complete each order manually by shipping the products to each consumer who has placed an order on your website. It's that simple! If you can run your own home, you can run your own business. It's not rocket science. If you can't do all the work yourself and there isn't enough time in the day to complete all the tasks required, then just hire staff to help run your business. After all, it is all about team work. You just need good leadership qualities and business management skills to run a successful enterprise.

Good Customer Service

Once, your Music Portal is up and running, you will also need to provide great customer service almost 24 hours per day, 7 days per week (especially if you are selling music and merchandise to a global market). However, you can stipulate your office opening and closing times on your website and provide customers with a way of contacting you via email when you are away from the office, so that you can respond to any customer service queries as soon as possible. You can also provide an office phone number and allow customers to leave messages. I would recommend that you respond to customers as quick as possible. Ideally, within an hour or so, or within a few hours. And at the very least within 24 hours. If it's taking you too long to process orders and deal with customers and respond to customer service queries, then it sounds like you have too much workload and it would be advisory that you hire someone to provide customer service on a part-time or full-time basis. This will leave you free to focus on other business activities such as making music or other day to day management activities of your business.

A Music Portal of the 21st Century is a portal for a worldwide audience. It gives fans or anyone using the internet, access to your music anywhere in the world at any time of the day. It is a permanent advert for all your music releases. Whether that be if they're searching for information about the artist or band; or information about a music release; or finding out when the artist or band is doing a tour. Fans can buy your music direct from you using online media. So, you will need to provide great customer service and constantly strive to improve the customer experience of your Music Portal. You are not just running a record label and distributing your music. You are also dealing with the retail side of the business and will need good customer service skills and experience to deal with customers on a daily basis. This in itself can be very time consuming. So make sure you have someone to fill this role. Depending on how many customer service queries you receive on a daily basis, it may be that you need to hire more than one person in a customer service role and recruit employees who speak several languages. Customers will come from all over the world and you will need to be ready and prepared to deal with any queries.

Sell and Distribute your own Music

The most common way of selling music is getting music releases stocked in as many shops/stores as achievable including online retail to get as much visibility as possible. Physical products have always had the advantage of staying fresh in people's minds when they've visited a shop or store. It is great advertising for your product/s. If your album is visible in a supermarket, then chances are they might buy it on the second or third visit to the store. This is a key element in the marketing of an artist or band's music. If you visit Spotify, the chances of you discovering new music is very slim unless you happen to come across it on a playlist. If a customer visits a shop and sees an album on display on the shelf or on the front page of the website, then they are more likely to take notice of that artist in the future and check out their music. It's also possible to have a playlist on your website with new releases playing automatically in the background.

It can be a logistical nightmare distributing your music releases to as many shops/stores as you can unless you use a distribution company who have years of experience in this field. Sometimes, it is really difficult to get your music stocked in some retailers as everyone is fighting for shelf space and competition is fierce. Some retailers won't even stock your music releases unless they are projected to sell hundreds of thousands of copies or more and if you are investing lots into marketing the music. Record shops are closing all the time too. It makes things even more complicated. This is why you will need a Music Portal of your own or to be affiliated to a Music Portal, so that you can get your music releases stocked both online and in shops/stores on the high street. You would usually need an endless supply of cash to remain competitive and stay ahead of everyone else and get your music stocked in all the right places. If you are selling your own music on your own Music Portal on the internet, then you do not need to distribute your music to any other retailers but your own. This makes the whole process a lot more straightforward. It will also save you a lot of expense.

If you choose to sell your music exclusively or non-exclusively on your own Music Portal, it is entirely up to you! The more people selling your music, the more sales there will be. But if you sell music releases exclusively on your own Music Portal, then fans will have to buy music releases directly from you and no one else. This will help generate a lot more traffic to your website and you may be able to sell advertising space which would be an additional revenue stream. A Music Portal is in simple terms, a fusion of an Online Shop/Store, Distributor and a Record Label all rolled into one. Everything is done in-house including the physical and digital distribution of any music releases. The only thing you may need is physical storage space to store all the physical products you are selling until they have been shipped out to customers. But if you are operating a pre-order only business model, then this won't be too much of a problem. It's not like you're going to be pressing up hundreds of thousands or millions of copies of a music release and need a warehouse to store them all in until they've been shipped to the customers.

There is no requirement to get your music stocked in all the shops on a nationwide scale or internationally and physically distribute it to them which is a logistical nightmare. Fans just type in a few key words on search engines such as Google or Bing and then click on the link to visit your Music Portal or a Music Portal you are affiliated with. Within minutes, they will be able to find your website and preview any music releases and then order goods from your Portal. You don't even need to press up thousands or millions of copies of your records anymore either. So, there goes the need for Record Companies to mass produce your music. You can take pre-orders instead at first and then press up the exact amount of copies required thus saving you a lot of money and decreasing your chances of going bankrupt. This is the most cost-effective way of running a business in the 21st century. The pre-order business model doesn't just apply to the music industry but also to other industries too. I predict many businesses will use the pre-order business model where practical in the future which will be much more friendlier to the environment and will keep costs down immensely and ensure the survival of a lot of businesses. Remember, it's all about meeting demand with the right amount of supply. Not the other way around. There is no point in having surplus copies of records taking up important storage space.

It may not be the answer to your prayers having your own Music Portal, but it will certainly help you overcome any obstacles when trying to get your music into the retail side of the music business. You will increase your chances of getting paid by the fans and they will know that the right people are getting paid as opposed to all the crooks who currently work in the record industry. As I have explained before, you will need quality music to be truly successful in the music business, but taking over the distribution side of your music and covering the retail side will give you more control over the distribution, from the second you master the final version of your tracks in the recording studio to making a digital copy and distributing it to anyone. Running your own Music Portal means that you will have to take responsibility for all aspects of the business. Just like a traditional record label would handle all your business affairs, from pressing and manufacturing your music on to CD and Vinyl and organizing tours. You will need to do the same.

If you cover all the key areas of the business from manufacturing, marketing, distribution to retail, you will remove the requirement for third parties and using middlemen. You can build your own company. You can build your own team. You can become the boss. You will have full control over the income flow from the sales of records and merchandise etc. This is a key to success. Major Record Companies have their own distribution companies. They also own independent distribution companies that distribute independent record labels releases. They have the market cornered. They do everything in-house. This is why they're so successful and dominate the music business. I can't begin to stress how important this is and how crucial it is to your own success. We can build on the success that Major Record Companies have had in the past and learn from their trials and tribulations and pioneer music for future generations. We can make music for the 21st century and create our own platform for sharing our music with fans. Most importantly, we can ensure that everyone involved gets paid for their work, especially the musicians. Doing your own distribution and selling your own music is the way forward.

Expanding the Music Portal Concept

We should be calling the Record Companies of the future – Music Portals. Record Companies are old hat. They have had their day. The game is up so to speak. They no longer serve a purpose. Not from where I'm standing anyway. They no longer take risks and fund the recording of albums unless you're a superstar. Record labels were a thing of the twentieth-century and started to lose control at the start of the twenty-first century when illegal file sharing became a major problem. Napster kick started the revolution in the music industry. Ever since then, it has been a constant struggle and no one really knew which direction the music business was taking. They've tried everything and failed in my opinion. Music Portals take care of that side of the business now.

Music Portals are run by musicians. You either get with the program and adapt or get swept aside. Right now, there is a major battle going on for power and control over the music business and there is a considerable vacuum. Now, is the right time to put this new concept into action and develop it. I am already leading the way with my own Music Portal – Uplifted Music & Media Portal. Music Portals give fans access to information on artists and bands, they provide fans with information on new releases and tour dates and fans can purchase music releases and merchandise etc. direct from the portal. Music Portals merge everything into one. Why would a fan need to listen to music on a streaming platform and keep renewing their subscription when they can preview music releases on the Music Portal which is home to the artists instead? They should be coming to us to listen to our music, not third parties!

There is nothing to stop you having your own bricks and mortar record shop/store and office premises for your Music Portal on the high street. Obviously, this will depend on your finances at the time. But there is room for expansion and major development. As more and more retailers close their businesses, this is your chance to fill the gap in the market and launch the futuristic record companies of the 21st century. It would be like a one-stop shop. There is nothing to prevent you from having a chain of Music Portals on the high street under the same name. It would be highly effective and bring advertising costs down as everyone involved in the chain of Music Portals on the high street would be marketed under the one company name and same adverts. This would help reduce marketing costs dramatically and make one page adverts more affordable by sharing the costs. By grouping together you would have a much higher chance of success. The Music Portal may even have a presence on the high street in more than one city or town. There may be several of them or a chain of Music Portals up and down the country all operating under the same group name. You could expand further by going international and setting up Music Portals under the same group name in other countries around the world.

One thing you need to be clear with from the beginning is that Music Portals aren't going to guarantee you any sales of your records. That is one of the greatest misconceptions of the music industry. Everyone thinks that you just need to make a record and it will sell. I'm sorry to tell you this. But it doesn't work like that. It's not that straightforward! You have to have a good marketing plan in place and quality music to do that. It also takes a lot of luck. But it will guarantee that you do get paid if you do generate sales as you will either own or co-own the Music Portal as part of a co-operative or you will be affiliated to it in some way or another. The idea behind Music Portals is that they are owned and run by musicians who have a passion for music. It is about musicians having more of an influence in the music business and getting more involved in the industry side of things, rather than rely on third parties to look after business affairs.

You will no longer have to go through a long line of middlemen. It is basically the artist or record label taking back control of the music business and taking back the power and covering all angles themselves. It is about becoming more efficient and running a much more profitable business which takes less financial risks, keeps costs down and to a minimum and reinvests profits back into the music community and develops the artists of tomorrow. The DJ's and the rest of the music industry have had it good for far too long. All these steps put the balance of power back firmly with the musicians and creators of the music. Everyone else has been getting paid through work directly or indirectly involved with creative people, namely musicians. And the majority of the time, it's been the musicians that have had to struggle and suffer throughout life. Music Portals will change all this. Musicians have to become better businessmen and women in order to survive. It's the only way you'll ever become successful!

In-store performances might take place in some of the high street Music Portals to help promote new releases. There may be single, album, book and poster signing sessions. Fans will be able to pre-order new releases in advance of their release in the bricks and mortar versions of the Music Portals by completing a pre-order form in-store or online and paying there and then. Fans could be able to pay in cash or by credit/debit card or even gift cards. They will be able to preview new music releases in-store at listening posts. They will be able to listen to new music releases on the in-store radio station that is playing in the background whilst fans browse through records in stock in the shop/store on the high street.

Customers in the bricks and mortar version of the Music Portal can access the Online version of the Music Portal on numerous desktop computers and preview new releases on the website and make a pre-order and pay online or pay at the cashier desk. Music Portals on the high street could stock old releases from artists and bands affiliated to the Music Portal and also music releases from third parties. Music Portals on the street could stock physical copies of music releases from the past and present. They could also sell instant downloads and copies of mp3's and fans could copy files on to a USB Flash Drive which the customer has brought with them or transfer it onto their mobile phones within minutes and purchase an appropriate end user license to do this. The list of options is endless. I am merely suggesting ideas and brainstorming.

The Music Portal on the high street could be a futuristic shop with internet access that serves drinks and refreshments. Similar to a coffee shop/internet café. This would encourage music lovers to interact and socialize more with each other instead of chatting online to each other over social media platforms such as Facebook which is killing society and it would be a place for them to meet up and have a chat and then browse through what new music releases are available. It would be a way for fans to develop relationships and talk about music and their favourite artists and bands and discuss whatever topic they feel like talking about. Fans could have face to face contact with representatives of the Music Portal rather than dealing with a faceless company such as Spotify.

Another suggestion would be to expand the online version of the Music Portal by including a forum for fans to connect with each other. The Music Portal would need public liability insurance and to adhere to health and safety rules if it were to become like an internet café. But it would create more additional revenue streams and be the number one place for music fans to converge. These are just suggestions of course, but you will get the general idea of how we can expand the Music Portal concept and cover many different areas of business. So, you could in theory sell food and drinks and snacks. You could also sell tickets for gigs, merchandise, DVD's, Blu-Rays, books and magazines in the bricks and mortar version of the Music Portal. Whatever you can think of that would be appropriate in a Music Portal, then do it.

If you can sell your music releases directly to fans, it may be that you will need to consider putting on your own live events in the future too which could also be a problem. I mean this because sometimes it is difficult to rent venues in the locations where your fans are based or it may be difficult to get a gig due to the politics that exist within the music industry or even mobilize a team to help put on an event. Some concert venues are owned by corporations within the music industry which makes it arduous to get to hire the venue you would like to play at and put on a gig which would cater for the demand in the local area where your fans are based. It may be that you have to buy a venue in order to put live events on or build a new concert venue in a certain city or town. There are always ways around any obstacles that get in your way. You can also sell tickets for gigs through your own Music Portal which is another lucrative revenue stream. The live sector of the music industry is definitely worth considering getting involved in. It comes hand in hand with making and selling music.

There's nothing to stop you doing many deals with third parties and licensing other retailers to sell your music digitally and on physical formats. You could do this all on the pre-order business model. Other retailers could pre-order a certain amount of copies of your music releases on physical formats and sell them in their own retail stores both online and offline. This will increase your sales tenfold. A Music Portal is a combination of all the main elements in the traditional sales model. Everything in one box. Even people in space will be able to access our music 24/7 and even order copies and have them delivered digitally or physically to a space hotel in a hundred years in the future, overlooking the stars in a mesmerizingly colourful and beautiful background and spiritually awakening atmosphere. You may have to consider distributing your music releases to other solar systems in the future as soon as we have conquered space travel and the ability to travel at the speed of light or faster than the speed of light. You may find yourself having to start a Music Portal on another planet in another solar system! Maybe I'm jumping the gun a bit too much? But it's all about having a vision for the future and being more forward thinking.

There is no need for third party distributors anymore. You can take care of the distribution yourself to retain all your rights and exploit them in the ways which you see fit. Distributing music releases yourself could become a job in itself, not just for one person but for a whole company of employees or partners. You will be in a better position to help those close to you. You will be able to create employment for you, your family and friends. It's what you can do for the local and international community that is of great benefit. It will help give people a purpose in life and it will create jobs, improve the local economy and open up many doors. Perhaps, you will create an inter-galactic chain of Music Portals in the future and music will truly become the universal language. If only we had a crystal ball!

Running your own business comes with extra responsibilities

You will have the added responsibility of managing your business and processing orders and distributing music releases and merchandise etc. to fans. So, if you don't have enough time in the day to multi-task then you may have to consider employing an assistant on a part-time or full-time basis. If you're receiving more sales than you anticipate, there isn't going to be enough time to do everything yourself if you're also the one making the music, practicing and rehearsing for gigs. You need to remember it's all about team work. That's how you become successful in anything. Owning and running your own Music Portal brings on many extra responsibilities. It may be physically impossible to do everything yourself. You may have to decide whether it's being an artist you love doing or running a successful business. But you will be in a better position financially and you will be able to pick and build your own team. It's all about taking responsibility for your own business affairs. Don't rely on third parties to look after you, as they will only let you down and by the time you've realized, it will be too late!

If you do not want extra responsibilities then it may be wise to get your music stocked in other retailers and let them manage your business affairs and sort the distribution out for you. But remember with a Music Portal of your own, visitors to your site can read about their favourite artists and bands and instantly check out information about their new releases and then click on another link to order their music on physical formats and buy merchandise. They can also find information about live gigs coming up in the future and order tickets direct from the Music Portal. Why other record labels and shops are not already doing this is anyone's guess? May be they already are! Just we don't see it. Or maybe they're not that forward thinking and adapting to the times. Well don't worry! Us artists are leading the way.

What formats to sell on the online version and high street version of the Music Portal

By selling your music on a Music Portal or Music Portals, you will be able to sell music releases on CD, Vinyl, Cassette Tape and in new digital formats such as WAV Format on USB Flash Drives which can come with a plastic tray and inlay for artwork, information and lyrics. You could still sell digital downloads such as mp3's and make them available for instant download. But this would mean that you would need more web space on the server hosting your Music Portal on the internet to store all your music files. However, with WAV Format (which is a higher quality digital audio recording of the music) you can include licensing agreements in pdf format which explain the terms and conditions of the purchase and which restrict licensed end users from making any more digital copies of music releases than necessary. You will also be able to sell merchandise on your online shop/store which is another important revenue stream. If you just sell physical and tangible goods on your website, you will not need instant downloads and you won't have to pay for additional web space to store all your digital music files. You will also decrease the chances of people hacking into your site to steal copies of your music in digital format as you are only selling physical products. You could sell the same physical formats in the high street version of the Music Portal too.

Taking orders for copies of your music to be pressed up on to CD, Vinyl and WAV Format on a pre-order basis and business model is the best way forward as it reduces financial risk and you meet demand with the right amount of supply. There's less chance of ending up bankrupt and in dire straits as I've explained before. What's the point in pressing a million copies of a record and only selling 10,000 units? The only people that benefit from this outdated business model is the pressing and duplication plants. It's not in your best interests to keep making the same mistakes as other record companies have done in the past. This also applies to merchandise and ticket sales etc. It's economical, friendly to the environment, cuts out all the middlemen and deals directly with the fans. This is the best solution in the 21st century for music retail.

I can imagine many other industries will catch on to this and start implementing pre-order only business models in the future. I'm not so sure about the food and drinks industry. But for the entertainment industry it may prove to be much more of an efficient way of doing business. Far too many businesses end up bankrupt and never last more than 10-20 years. Especially businesses on the high street. In the forty or so years that I've lived on planet Earth, I've seen many changes on the high street. The pre-order business model is one way to avert disaster. Other third party retailers could purchase copies of your music releases if you want to involve third parties using the pre-order business model. This would guarantee you sales. Or alternatively, they could take pre-orders on your behalf. You can sell to online shops or record stores on the high street and increase sales this way. The main advantage of owning your own Music Portal is that you can sell your own music as a backup plan if all else should fail. This is the true meaning of independence.

You don't even need to own your own Music Portal. You could work with an existing website and partner up with them if they are looking to stock other music releases. Just do a licensing deal with them or get them to take pre-orders on your behalf. The more sales you can get, the better really in order to cover all your costs and put on events. You can organize your own events and sell music and merchandise at gigs and also hand out forms to fans so that they can order products from you online. You don't have to do it all completely independent. You can still work with third parties but only work with reputable firms. The Music Portal is a concept. It's still in its infancy. As I've said before, these are all just suggestions. I could possibly write a whole book on the subject of Music Portals and go in to great detail about it all.

You can also add direct links to visit the order page on the Online Shop/Store of a product or various products. Don't forget to include pictures of the artists and bands and biographies on the main part of the website for your Music Portal. Don't overwhelm visitors to your website with too much information and too many menus. Keep it nice and simple. People only have a finite amount of time to navigate through your website to find the information they are searching for. Less is more.

The amount of information you can include on a Music Portal is endless. You can also sell advertising space on a Music Portal and create additional revenue streams. If one or more of your music releases happens to be very popular it will attract more traffic to the website which will in turn motivate advertisers to place something about their own product on the Music Portal. You may also be able to offer sponsorship opportunities to local businesses and international companies. Just imagine one day in the future you may be in a position to sign new artists and bands to your own Music Portal and help them if they aren't in a position to do it themselves! But remember to be honest and transparent with them and help them. Reputation is everything!

The amount of things you can do with a Music Portal is also unlimited. I've tried my very best to list as many ideas as possible in this chapter. You now know that as well as having an online presence you could also consider having a visible presence on the high street and a chain of Music Portals throughout the nation or you could expand further and go global or even inter-galactic for that matter. Music videos and audio clips can be included on Music Portals both online and in-store to help promote music releases and you can include links to social media accounts. Or maybe in the future it will be possible to have a social networking platform integrated into your online version of your Music Portal so fans can connect instantly with one another and discuss new music or attending a gig together.

The general idea behind the Music Portal is to put the power and control back with the creators of the music. It is in our best interests to save the music industry and lead the way and help develop it for future generations. It is also to help create a place where music lovers and fans alike can meet and socialize and develop friendships and relationships. We rely far too heavily on the virtual world at the moment and it is destroying societies. People are becoming more and more anti-social and there is less real interaction in the 21st century. I don't want to deal with faceless companies such as Spotify and pay more than I have to just to rent music as opposed to owning a copy. I prefer the old way. It worked fine until the internet came along. Now I'm adapting to the worldwide web and making the best of it. You can too if you want to. These are the blueprints for a Music Portal.

In the next chapter, I discuss general tips and advice about the music industry from my own personal experiences over the last two decades. I hope this chapter on Music Portals helps you a lot and gets you thinking about the future of the music business and increases your confidence and self-belief and gives you more faith that you can be successful in the music industry if you cover all the angles from manufacturing, marketing, distribution to retail.

7

GENERAL MUSIC INDUSTRY TIPS AND ADVICE

In this chapter, I would like to share many tips and advice with you about the music industry. Stuff which they don't teach you at school, college or university. I wish someone had told me all these things when I was young and naïve and not very clued up on the business side of the music industry. Ideally, I could have done with a manager to look after my business affairs. But in all honesty, I was always unmanageable. I'm very independent and used to working on my own and looking after myself. So, that's probably why I never attempted to search for a manager! I'm sure I'm not the only one.

There are things you can do to help yourself such as reading plenty of books about the music business, especially autobiographies written by other artists and bands and my book for example. You can also watch documentaries and videos and also hire a manager and a lawyer who has plenty of experience in the music industry and someone who is honest and trustworthy and who will get you the best deals and most importantly look after your best interests. I will start this chapter off by giving you some examples of incidents that happened to me at the start of my electronic dance music career and modern day issues with downloading and streaming and other important topics.

License your music

Digital music content only works for artists and bands if they're getting paid for the right to exploit their music in that way. You need to license your music to third party digital music content platforms as opposed to waiting for royalties from sales. Whether that's downloading or streaming, you need to write up a licensing agreement on your terms and get any third parties to sign and date it before handing over any master copies of your music to them. You can either write up an agreement yourself or get a music lawyer to help with it. Do not hand over any copies of your music to any third parties until you have received a copy of the licensing agreement back from them with a date and signature on it and also an advance payment. If they pay you by cheque/check, please ensure it clears first before you distribute your music to them.

Digital downloads and streaming are open to abuse and corruption with no real way of knowing whether statements produced on excel spreadsheets are genuine and that they have not been tampered with or changed to suit those services and to make it look like you've had less sales or streams than you may have done. It is much better to license your music to these third party platforms in the form of a digital music content licensing agreement. Instead of waiting for royalties from sales or streams of your music, it is much more preferable to ask for an advance licensing fee and monthly licensing fees irrespective of how many downloads or streams your music gets.

Corruption is rife in the music industry

Some artists and bands or record labels or people use software to manipulate the number of streams on services like Spotify (an online digital music jukebox) which creates more royalties for them. There are all kinds of scams that go on in the music industry. Not all is what it seems! We cannot really trust anything we read or see. Some people create the illusion that they are more successful than they actually are in reality. For instance, DJ's in the electronic dance music scene use ghost producers to make it appear as though they are writing and producing music themselves so that they receive all the credit for it.

There is an awful lot of corruption that goes on in the music industry, especially the dance music scene! I would love to name some examples of the perpetrators but I will avoid doing this to avoid any court cases and let you find out for yourselves. A lot of the culprits are well known established DJ's. In fact, they've been considered Superstar DJ's. It's common knowledge within inner circles of the dance music business as to who they are. More often than not, it's those DJ's who have money and who belong to the aristocracy.

The only reason they appear to be so successful is because they are being bankrolled by the banks or by private investors or they are rich to begin with! So, please don't get too disappointed when you eventually realize that scenes like the dance music business are fixed and there is no hope of ever really being successful and making it big and becoming a superstar DJ yourself. I have done a lot of research on this very subject and discovered a lot of revelations. You can usually spot the DJ's that are aristocracy from Holland or Germany by their surnames. They usually have names like "Van" or "Von" in their surnames. Do the research yourself if you don't believe me!

Digital content has devalued music

Downloading and streaming has devalued music in the last decade. For a start mp3's and streaming formats are low quality audio recordings of your music and add no value to your music whatsoever. Hence, why if I release new music it will only be on CD and vinyl and future physical mediums and on a pre-order basis only. I will never distribute master copies of the music to anyone or press any copies up for anyone else but myself unless they make a pre-order from my own music portal or a trusted source. It makes better business sense to do it this way and saves you from getting into any debt or ending up bankrupt as I did when I pressed up my debut album – Vitality "Vitality" on my first record label – TSYT RECORDINGS in 2004.

Only I will have my music in my possession and only I will play it out live as an artist or DJ unless third party DJ's buy promo copies of my music in advance of their official pre-order release dates and are licensed to use them in public performances. I'm not too bothered whether people order my music or not. I'm happy enough with copies of my music just for myself which I can play on a turntable at home. That way there's no financial risk involved and having surplus copies of records I can't shift. It makes much better sense to do it that way. I advise other musicians, artists and bands to do exactly the same.

any third parties such as streaming services like Spotify who want copies of the music would have to have a licensing agreement in place with me on my terms. They would have to pay me an advance licensing fee and monthly digital music content licensing fees. It makes much better business practice! I spoke with a member of the European Parliament recently on the issue of digital music content on third party download and streaming services. I put forward the suggestion of artists and bands licensing their music instead of waiting to receive royalties from these services as the chances are they will never get paid. Hopefully, the issue will be addressed. Ideally, there needs to be a streaming law as opposed to a copyright law but we can't wait around for those in power to get their act together.

Dirty tricks

Some people use smear campaigns against artists and bands as a way to affect sales of their music in a negative way. They will make false allegations against you or spread false rumours. All kinds of dirty tricks are used in the music business. It doesn't just happen in the music business, but also normal life and in many other industries. I learnt this as I got older. It's best you know this information now to know what to look out for and to avoid certain situations which may make you vulnerable and put you in an uncompromising position. I know it's the rock and roll thing to do, but try to avoid jumping into bed with total strangers as people will use honeytraps to lure you in to situations. They will try to extract information from you or set you up for a major fall. Get to know people well first and find out about their background before you provide them with any bits of information which they might try to use against you.

I have enough shit to deal with in my life as it is. I often receive abuse both online and offline. It never used to be like this until I started producing electronic dance music and DJ'ing. More often than not, it is jealousy and envy, but sometimes it is competition from within the music industry. People will befriend you and smile to your face. But secretly, they hate you and are your enemy. This is the reality of the music business. I can count my real friends on one hand. Most people in the business are acquaintances. So, don't be too despondent when you discover not everyone is your friend or ally. There are a lot of snakes out there who want a share of the pie and they'll do and say anything to get it. It's a cut throat industry. That famous saying is very true! So, you have to have very thick skin to deal with all that is thrown at you.

Surround yourself with trustworthy people

Be wary of people who try to get you to take various drugs. More often than not, it can lead to mental health problems and addictions which are designed to curtail your music career. Don't listen to people who are plastic surgeons. You are beautiful the way you are. They are only interested in your money (not that most of us have any), so will say anything to you to get you to pay them to do work on your face and they will prey on your insecurities. I never had a problem with this but there are people out there who will gladly encourage you to have a nose job or lip job and then make you look completely plastic and not as good looking as you were to begin with. They are very manipulative people.

This is why it's so important to have family and close friends around you who you can trust and who will give you an honest opinion. Your physical appearance isn't the be all and end all. God loves you the way you are! So, learn to love yourself in the skin you are in before you enter the limelight. Far too many sensitive souls have died as a result of this in the music business. I think you know who I am talking about! A certain famous American Motown and Pop artist who died a few years ago springs to mind.

Legal loopholes

The PRS For Music which is a royalty collecting society, which I am currently a member of at the time I am writing this book, does not really seem to represent all of its members and does not seem capable of understanding how streaming is not much different to downloading. They have allowed streaming services like Spotify to get away without ever having to pay any mechanical royalties despite music being uploaded to their servers and copies made before end users have streamed any music from their streaming platform. Uploading and downloading is all pretty much the same. I don't think there is any real difference between downloading a song and making a copy it, than streaming music. It's all the same to me. It's just a legal loophole.

It's a constant struggle

It has seemed a constant struggle throughout my life to get full time work and get paid no matter what I do. I seem to be persecuted a lot. I get a lot of grief and abuse from people not just online but offline as well. I keep myself to myself and rarely go out and have a very small and close circle of friends that I can count on one hand. It's better that way. A lot safer for me and much more secure. Avoid the party scene like the plague if you can and lead a quiet, private, healthy and balanced life away from the media and spotlight. It's the best advice I can give you to ensure that you keep your sanity intact. You have to be very security conscious. You also have to be strong and take no shit from anyone!

Royalty statements

Even royalty statements from all the record labels in the past I was signed to such as Source Of Gravity Records, Gravitation, Baroque Records, Method Records, Three (3 Beat) and Mechanism Recordings etc. never disclosed how much money they were paying themselves. Not once was i ever disclosed. For example: Baroque Records were selling 2000 copies of my records at an average of £6 per copy. That's a revenue of £12,000. We got paid £750 for Evenflow "Indecisive which I shared with Gary Morris. I received just £375 for that track which I wrote and produced mostly and it got played at Cream in Liverpool which was a super club at the time and was one of my biggest hits. So, how much did they earn from that particular release not to mention the others? I never even received a copy of the royalty statement for my track Source Of Gravity "Perseverance" which I co-wrote with Chris Steriopulos.

always expected to receive royalties from sales of records but the record labels always found a way of extorting any money that was due to me as an artist by coming up with preposterous fees such as "website update"! They'll try and charge you for anything they can and pass the costs on to you as the artist as though you are the customer which is completely ridiculous and wrong. That's why I advise you not to take expensive private jets and chauffeur driven limousines when you're travelling around the world when you're touring if you are signed to a major record label or any record label in fact.

This is one of the biggest reasons as to why I had major financial difficulties and ended up bankrupt because of the knock on effect of never having received much in the way of an income from my music career. No doubt, all these record label bosses were snorting the proceeds from the sales of my records up their noses and hiring prostitutes! It would not surprise me one bit. I went through an awful lot of stress during that time. I hope God deals with them in the afterlife, not in this life. After all, greed is a sin.

itality "Skylite" released on Keith McDonnell's – Method Records based in Coventry, UK in 2003 - I received just £250! Yet again how much did they draw in wages or fees for that release? I was majorly exploited. The likes of James Holden who was also a rising star in the Progressive House/Trance music scene at the same time was getting paid a few thousand for his releases on record labels that he was signed to. Chris Steriopulos of Source Of Gravity Records also paid jade - £2000 for a remix of my track when I needed it more to pay the bills for the equipment I was buying to produce the records. Back then, the only thing that kept me going was my sound production business and working other jobs. The contracts I was signing with these labels weren't worth the paper they were written on.

o, as you can imagine, no wonder I have ill feeling towards the so called "Progressive House" music scene. Most of the DJ's and record labels are a bunch of criminals pulling scam after scam and there is no transparency whatsoever with the statements that they produce for artists on their roster. I would not be surprised if one day artists and bands hire hitmen to have them all bumped off. People seem to think they can screw artists and bands over left, right and centre without any comeback until they mess with the wrong people. Karma has a funny way of reaching people and delivering karma. I personally would not feel any sadness or sympathy for any of them if it were to happen. I guess it's never too late to confess their sins?

There is no money in digital music for artists

owadays, with regards to digital music, there's no money in it whatsoever. It just isn't feasible r worthwhile to do it. People have no respect for digital music content and the creators of music especially in digital format. Whereas digital music is concerned, there is zero respect for intellectual property. It was a shame to part company with record labels like Source Of Gravity Records but I got the impression they used my music solely to promote their record labels using the Source Of Gravity artist name and brand.

They also used my releases to get DJ gigs for themselves through those releases and build up their own business. They were not interested in my welfare or paying me the going rates or in promoting me. I took the majority of the financial risk by purchasing all the equipment for my studio to produce the electronic dance music which they needed to use when DJ'ing at gigs. It was all about them. The dance music scene is a law unto itself and they don't really care about the artists that they exploit.

Chris Steriopulos of Source Of Gravity Records in the Isle Of Man took little financial risk by having a pressing and distribution deal with Unique Distribution which was based in Bolton, Greater Manchester at the time, without ever consulting me or letting me see the details of the deal he had in place with them. This all happened whilst I was travelling around West Virginia in America in 2000. It just led to a complete lack of trust. I eventually asked him to stop using the Source Of Gravity name a few years back and he now uses the name "Soundscapes Digital". Although, he gave me my first break with regards to getting my music released, I'd be very wary of unscrupulous business men like him. It would seem he knew exactly what he was doing from the beginning!

Why musicians are always poor!

Have you ever wondered why so many other people but musicians can afford to go on regular holidays all the time all around the world and afford luxury yachts? Well, it's most likely because of all the money they have made from shares in oil companies and major record companies and the sales from music releases which they've pocketed. It's the musicians money that they've been spending! That's why most musicians are poor and struggle throughout life. We get a very bad deal from it all. That's my conclusion. Only the oil companies, shareholders, vinyl and CD pressing plants benefit from music being pressed on to vinyl or CD as it is the plastic which is used. Oil is used to make the plastic. The oil companies are all a bunch of crooks as we already know.

They are on to a winner with those formats as it doesn't matter how many copies of your records are sold as they make a profit regardless. No wonder they are so rich! That's why they used to encourage musicians to release music all the time on vinyl and CD formats on record labels even if not all copies of a record were sold. It was a win-win situation for them. This is why I recommend we as musicians, artists and bands start taking pre-orders only for our releases to minimize financial risk and to stop making oil companies super rich. It's also better for the environment in which we live.

I believe one of the main reasons why they keep musicians poor is to get us to keep making new songs and doing tours to keep the money rolling in for those who are extorting and pocketing all the income from the sales of records and from ticket sales for gigs. If we made enough money to retire on after one album, we probably wouldn't need to make any more music and could retire. But those in power don't want this to happen so there is a constant stream of income coming in for them to pay for their mansions and all their holidays and luxury yachts whilst we do all the hard work and graft.

People in the music industry and also some of the public expect artists and bands to work for free and do it for the love of it whilst everyone else gets paid. The mentality and attitudes towards musicians stinks and in general is outrageous and disgraceful. It's also immoral to treat people like slaves in the 21st century. This has to stop and things have to change. Consumers attitudes and behaviour towards musicians need to change as well.

As musicians, we often hear people telling us to "do it for the love of it" which we already do. I find this very insulting. But what if we turned things upside down and started telling other people in other industries such as Doctors, Nurses, Police, Army, Politicians, Firemen, Lawyers, Football Coaches, Football players and Architects etc. to start doing it for the love of it too? What if we told them to work for free and to never get paid for their work? They wouldn't like it either! So, why on earth is there still discrimination against anyone involved in making music in the 21st century?

License your music to third party DJ's

Professional DJ's who are classed as third parties should pay DJ license fees to artists and bands directly instead of paying organisations such as the PRS For Music which is a royalty collecting society for a DJ license. Middlemen are a cancer to the music industry. It is possible to recruit your own team of in-house DJ's who can help promote your music without needing a third party license to do it. But any third parties need to be licensed to use our music in public performances. This is a vital source of income for all artists and bands. This is another issue which needs addressing.

Don't upload your music

We do not have to wait for any laws to be passed regarding copyright law to prevent third party digital music content platforms such as the controversial streaming service – Spotify from exploiting our music. We simply just need to avoid uploading our music to these third party digital music content platforms in the first place. We need to write up a "contract" of our own. In other words, create our own digital music content licensing agreements written on our terms so that it benefits us as opposed to everyone else. This legally binding document will stand in our favour in a court of law especially if there is a breach of contract. Once, a third party digital music content platform signs the licensing agreement and pays a fee in advance to us for the right to exploit our music, distribute it and sell it, we can then upload or distribute our music to them without any problems arising.

As part of any licensing deal/agreement which we or our specialist music lawyers write up, we can then charge third party digital music content platforms a regular monthly/yearly licensing fee which they must pay to us promptly and on time. Failure to do so, would be a breach of contract and would result in us removing our music content from their services. If they do not abide by the contract, then the licensing deal becomes void and invalid. They would need to remove our music from their digital music content sharing platforms. We would also have the option then to take legal action against them and sue them in a court of law.

So, to sum it all up. We do not need to wait for streaming laws to be passed or for reform on copyright laws. The power is with us. We simply do not upload or distribute our music to digital distributors/aggregators/third party digital music content platforms in the first place until they have signed and agreed to a licensing deal with us on our terms and have paid an advance licensing fee upfront! If we take these steps it will improve things drastically. The major record companies already have licensing deals in place with companies such as Spotify. So, why are we not doing this?

Form a breakaway music league

The whole business model for the music industry is currently set up to make everyone but the musicians wealthy. We need to create a new business model and form a breakaway league and also form an international musician's union with legal representation. There is nothing to stop us all from forming our own company and all becoming members. We could start our own Plc (Public Limited Company) and issue shares to the public as a way of raising the funds required to produce and release music and to also put tours on around the world. There is nothing to stop us from forming our own major record companies. It's not as difficult as you think. I know how to do it myself. It just takes a team effort and a lot of organization. The next chapter in my book explains exactly how to go about doing this.

The music industry is extremely corrupt. It is full of greedy, lazy and selfish people who treat artists and bands as unpaid or barely paid slaves. They treat artists as the customer. All of the record labels I was signed to did this to me when it came to accounting for music releases and producing royalty statements. They are simply motivated by the money aspect of it all. They certainly do not do it for the love of it. They are lying to you if they say they do. They are all hypocrites. So, take anything they say to you with a pinch of salt. They cannot be trusted one iota.

Introduce a new business model

Most people running the music industry do very little in the way of actual work. They are simply middlemen. We'd be better off hiring our family, friends and people from within our own communities who we know well and can trust to help us run our own futuristic record labels – Music Portals. Take a look at the illustration below to understand what I mean by middlemen:

The current Business Model

ARTIST > RECORD LABEL > DISTRIBUTOR > SHOPS > FANS

The Business Model of the future

ARTIST > MUSIC PORTAL > FANS

With the way things are right now and how it all currently works, music releases have to go through several middlemen before we even start to receive any income from sales of our music. Artists and bands are always last in line to get paid. The chances are by the time everyone has taken their slice of the pie, there is no income left for the artists. This is where the major problem is with the current business model. There is no need for all these middlemen and third parties to be involved in our music releases. There are ways of forming our own groups and working around these problems. We are just being scammed otherwise!

Competition

Another aspect about the music business which you might not know is that those artists and bands and DJ's that are already established in the music industry see other upcoming artists, bands and DJ's as competition and as a threat if you're not going through their middlemen and channels of distribution. They view others as stepping on their territory. It is a business to them. It is their livelihoods. It is all about the money to them no matter how much they try to deny it. So, they will say and do all kinds of things to manipulate you and make you feel bad.

They will only help you and play your music (especially the DJ's in the dance music scene) if they're making money from your music. They don't want you to make a living from music. They don't want you to take a slice of the pie as such. They want you to do it purely for the love of it. Otherwise, they view you as a major threat to them and as though you're trespassing on their property. That's why it's so difficult to make it in the music business and be successful. They'll even go as far as blockading your music and boycotting it. Hence, why it's so important to be independent and do everything in-house. It isn't really about the music with them. It's about money.

They will do and try anything to put a stop to your music career. I know this first hand because similar things happened to me over the last two decades. I learnt the hard way. However, I am much more wiser for it. I recommend you avoid the party scene as that is where you are more at risk and at your most vulnerable. Stick to making music and playing live. Stay focused and just do the job you love doing. Don't worry too much about having to be seen in public and networking. Leave that to the professionals. Just let things happen naturally.

Most of these established acts are part of a huge network and team backed by large financial institutions. So, they don't have your best interests at heart and want to see you fail. It's a tough industry to be in. I am not saying that all rival artists and bands are like this but a lot of them are. Always be aware of the wolves. It's usually their colleagues and friends who cause the most trouble for you when you're starting out and trying to become established in the music business.

Real music fans buy music and support artists

I strongly believe there will come a point where we have to counteract every move made by the music industry and some of the public. When I say "public" I refer to those that aren't real music fans and expect us to make music for free and the ones who don't ever want to pay for music and download our music from illegal file sharing services or make copies of our music illegally. We may have to stop giving copies of our music altogether to third party DJ's, Radio Stations, Record Companies and any other third parties in general. We will have to do everything completely in-house and boycott the industry and as I've mentioned before, it may be advisable to form our own breakaway music league.

The reason being for all of this is because it is becoming more and more apparent with each day that passes that our music (our intellectual property) creates jobs, employment and a regular income for everyone but ourselves. We as artists rarely get paid for our work. We do not seem to receive an income from our music. This is immoral and wrong and we are being majorly exploited as I've explained before. It can no longer continue and it is simply not sustainable. We have to teach all these people a very valuable lesson in life and boycott them all and do everything ourselves from plugging our music and promoting it to the real music fans who support us and respect us and love what we do. Why should everyone else get paid and not the musicians? We have to pay bills, put food on our tables and keep a roof over our heads.

Avoid being exploited

The mentality and attitude towards artists from people in the music industry is one of major exploitation. This either has to change and they have to show us some respect for them to earn our respect or otherwise they should change career and jobs themselves and find a new way of earning a living other than from cashing in on our intellectual property. We are not a charity. We do not have to entertain these people at all. We can sell our music on our own websites/shops/online stores (Music Portals). We can promote our own music ourselves on our own radio stations, in our own magazines and at gigs in an underground format and take pre-orders from fans to avoid any financial risk.

Take control of the distribution

We can do our own distribution. We can press up our own copies of our music on to vinyl and CD without taking any risk whatsoever. We can hire venues and put our own gigs and tours on together. We can help each other and work together as a brotherhood and as a community of like-minded musicians performing all the various roles. We will work much better as a team. We are stronger together. As a United Alliance we will have strength in numbers throughout the world. We will have strength in unity and strength in togetherness. If we do not do this and take the steps required to implement real change, then nothing will ever improve. The corruption and the exploitation will just carry on and most of us will live in poverty and misery for the rest of our lives and wonder where we went wrong and why we didn't do something about it.

Team work

Team work is the key to success. It is coming to the point where we need to stage a worldwide revolution within the music business. Without us (the musicians) there is no music industry. We have the power to change things for the better and improve the quality of our lives throughout the globe. The music industry is scared of losing control over all the artists and bands. They've been controlling us since the start of the recorded music industry. Before the recorded music industry started, the business thrived through music publishing by selling music manuscripts to other musicians to play classical music composers songs.

Take the power back

In basic terms, we need to take the power back and we need to do it now. Musicians have been scammed for far too long and have been treated very unfairly for a long time and we need to put an end to this major exploitation now. Even if it means going on strike and not ever giving any copies of our music to anyone and performing live for a while until we gain the respect we need. I realize this may be a difficult thing to do as we are so passionate about our music, but it makes better business sense to take this kind of action. The change we desire so much will never happen until we take serious action. We will continue to be a laughing stock and people will keep taking advantage of us.

I would never recommend a career in the music industry to any musicians. Especially, if we carry on adhering to the current business model. It simply does not work for the majority of musicians unless we are signed to a major record company and receiving a salary every year. I hope this chapter has been very helpful and informative. It has been a real eye opener for me in particular and I hope it has provided you with a massive insight into the workings of the music business and how corrupt it is. I am in no doubt that this will stand you in good stead for the rest of your life and give you an advantage in the future. You are less likely to make any mistakes or fall for any scams.

Blatant lies and deception

Chris Steriopulos, the so-called DJ friend who I met at university in about 1996/1997 who started his own Progressive House/Trance music record label – Source Of Gravity Records which was based in the Isle Of Man at the time, and released my first tracks told me not so long ago that he does music as a hobby. However, if you start selling music for commercial gain on download and streaming platforms, it is no longer considered as a hobby. This was a blatant lie.

He also has a music publishing deal with 23rd Precinct in Glasgow, Scotland for all of his latest music releases on his new record label – Soundscapes Digital. He is just one example of people who cannot be trusted who work in the music business. I will talk about this in more detail in a future book. In the next chapter of this book, I explain how to build your own music empire from scratch and describe all the constituent parts which are required to create a major record company.

8

HOW TO CREATE YOUR OWN MUSIC EMPIRE

So far, in this book, to recap on everything I have talked about, I have written about how I became involved in music from an early age to when I got my first record deal and beyond. I have explained ways in which you can market your music in the 21st century. I have discussed how to sell your music in challenging times. I have suggested ways in which you can get funding for your music projects and get the ball rolling. I have listed other sources of income which can provide additional revenue streams. I have described what a Music Portal is and how to incorporate all the various elements which help to create success in the music business in to one box. I've also provided general music industry tips and advice from my own experiences and other musicians experiences in the music business.

In all of the other chapters I have written about in this book on how to survive the music business and what to do and what not to do in order to increase your chances of success, I have talked about how to market your own music and all the pros and cons and pitfalls of working in the music industry from my own valuable experiences. The book has been full of tips and advice about the music industry in general and how to be very successful! However, in this chapter, I take a different direction and I help to give you a better understanding of how the music industry works and I focus on ways in which you as an entrepreneur can create your own destiny by building your own music empire. If you are interested in going that one step further and building your own major record company, then this chapter is definitely for you.

What is an empire you may ask? Well, an empire is an extensive group of states or countries ruled over by a single monarch, an oligarchy, or a sovereign state. In the case of the music industry, the big four – Universal Music Group, Sony BMG Music Entertainment, Warner Music Group and EMI Group spring to mind as current examples of music empires as they account for the most music sales globally and have the biggest market share. When I talk about empires, you might think of an empire which rules the world. Well, a music empire isn't much different. A music empire would rule the music industry. Empires are synonymous with things like the Roman and British Empires. So, in a way, building your own music empire is not much different to what a Roman Emperor would have done to create the Roman Empire. You literally have to think in the same way an emperor would in order to be hugely successful.

An empire can also be defined as an extensive sphere of activity controlled by one person or group. A music empire would cover certain territory around the world and have the most sales and the biggest market share like the existing four major record companies do. Your music empire would be based on a similar model to the other major record companies with a very similar infrastructure in place. By emulating the four major record companies as examples, you are more likely to be very successful. You can learn a lot from studying other successful businesses and how to avoid making simple mistakes. If you are seriously looking to build your own music empire, you must bear in mind that it will take a lot more than having a hit record. You will need to be consistent with every single music release from each artist and band which are signed to your major record company, not just some of the time, but all of the time.

I would suggest that you integrate the idea and concept of the Music Portal which I have talked about earlier in this book and extend it further in order to create your own music empire, the new type of record label for the 21st century. You can incorporate everything in to one box under the same group name or as a group of independent businesses working together and towards one goal. At the very minimum, you would at least require all of the following sectors: Record Labels, Music Publishing Company, Recording Studios, Music Magazines (physical and online), Music Venues for gigs, Radio Stations (FM, digital and online), TV Stations (Music Channels), Distribution Company, Retailers (High street shops/stores and online portals), Pressing and Duplication Plants and locations for annual outdoor festivals (see illustration below). These are the main requirements that you would need in order to build a successful music empire and it would help if you have a few million or billion pounds or dollars to spare and invest in the business. If you don't have the funds yourself, then it would help if you know someone or a group of wealthy people to help invest in the project. The only other option would be for everybody who is involved in the project to work together and volunteer until the business creates an income for everyone.

Empire Music Group
(Mother Company/Umbrella Group)

Record Label	Music Publishing Division	Radio Stations	TV Channels	Retailers	Distribution Company	Festivals

Sub Labels	Press (Music Magazines/Newspapers)		Music Venues		Pressing & Duplication Plants	

The music industry is very competitive and it is very difficult to get enough of a market share to make a living from music. So, you really do need to consider covering all angles. This chapter which I have written is also helpful for people who are interested in the music business and how it all works and ticks. It gives you a great insight in to the workings and mechanics of the music business and it will also help musicians to understand how much is involved in terms of time spent establishing the business, funding, infrastructure and personnel in order to be successful. It is like a do-it-yourself guide on how to establish a major record company in the 21st century. If you're a musician, it may either make you very cynical about the music business after reading this chapter or it will make you more knowledgeable and take things for granted a lot less than you used to do. Either way, it will give you a greater understanding of how everything works together and you will learn a lot more about the music industry and you will become very enlightened and it will stand you in good stead for the future.

This particular chapter is specifically written for music business minded and oriented people who want to create and run a prosperous music business in the 21st century using already established business models which the major record companies use. If you happen to have a few hundred million pounds or dollars (or whichever currency you choose to use) or make that billions spare to invest, you may want to consider creating your own music empire like in the illustration above. You will need to cover all the sectors of the music business and have departments for everything even if you outsource some of the work. You will require huge resources to make things happen. You will need human resources in every sector of the music business. The only way to run a successful organization is to cover all angles. Your music empire needs to invest in all the required parts or ingredients which make up an effective music business and which form the basis of the music industry. Don't worry if you don't have the capital required to form a major record company. You can always consider merging together with other companies to create a bigger company instead.

It would be a requirement for you to have your own music publishing division so that you can license music to third parties and also your own sub label's which cover all the different genres of music which you plan to release. It is necessary to have a constant flow of income coming in for your business from music releases which incorporates all the different genres. You have to cover every aspect of the music business and do as much as you can in-house. In theory, It's quite possible to do this without having any capital of your own to invest as I've already mentioned, but it will be a lot easier to buy up assets, hire personnel and then build your own infrastructure and put everything into place if you do possess the means to implement all of these strategies and take on all of my advice on how to set up and establish a major record company. By doing this, it will enable you to put together all the necessary elements which are required to create a profitable record company, market and promote all the acts on your roster.

In this chapter, I explain how to do this and also how to do it without any start-up capital. You don't need money to build your own empire, but believe me it helps. Especially, if you want to make it happen a lot faster! It's always possible to find a consortium of investors willing to invest in your project and to help raise the funds required to build your own music business by forming your own investment company or approaching venture capitalists to help fund the business and get it off the ground. This would be one way of getting started as an example. The investment company which you start up could be in the shape and form of a Limited Company or Plc (Public Limited Company) which would be its legal identity. The investment company you form is essentially a vehicle in which you use to buy up all the assets and hire personnel you need to create your own major record company and all the other parts needed to create a music empire.

There are many investment firms already out there such as Goldman Sachs which is an American multi-national investment bank as an example. Investment firms do what they say on the tin. They invest in other businesses and provide the funding to run a company and do what is necessary to make things happen. So, it is true, the banks do bankroll the majority of most artist and bands that are signed to major record companies! You could also form a parent company (umbrella company) and call it "Empire Music Group" for instance and merge several already established music businesses into one group under the parent company and work as a team as I have mentioned before. As a result of doing this and following my advice, your business will become a lot more efficient.

Investment firms already invest capital into well-established record companies as we know. Merging companies together is another way of doing it. I once wrote to EMI Music (UK) when I was the Managing Director of my first record company – TSYT RECORDINGS Ltd in about

2005/2006 and sent them a merger proposal. This was at a time when the music industry was in crisis with the development of the digital music revolution. Most people in the music industry didn't really understand what was going on and how to adapt to the situation. I had a very good idea about how to overcome these issues and decided to offer my services to other established businesses. Sometimes it pays dividends to approach other established businesses and work together with them by merging companies. Lots of companies do this all the time. Not many music industry executives had a good understanding of I.T. (Information Technology) and the internet, so at the time, it made perfect sense.

I considered myself as an expert at the time when I approached EMI Music (UK) with regards to the internet, information technology and computers and I still consider myself to be an expert to this very day. I also predicted the future of the music industry at the time with regards to downloads and streaming on an internet forum which I used to go on called "Global Underground". At the time it was called "pay-per-play". However, I was struggling financially myself after releasing my debut album Vitality "Vitality" on my record label - TSYT RECORDINGS and thought that I'd pitch my ideas to EMI Music (UK) as well as many other corporations and offer my services to them and suggest working as a team. As you may have gathered though, they didn't end up merging with my company and probably thought that I was some nutcase. At the time, it seemed like a sensible idea and the best way forward, but that's another story! Sometimes, it does no harm to give things a try. Never rule anything out.

Anyway, back to the subject I was discussing. Once, you have started your major record company, you can then start to consider looking for private investment as a limited company or for investment from the public as a Plc (Public limited company). You can do this by issuing new share capital and by selling shares in your company to any member of the public or any other companies or individuals. You do not need to be listed on the stock exchange to do this, but by floating on stock exchanges it will open up more doors for your business and generate external investment. You can create share capital and then issue shares in the millions to help raise the funds required to get your business off the ground. The danger of this though, is that another company could buy up the majority of the shares in your company and have more control over the way your business is run. This is a risk which you might have to take in order to establish your music business and acquire the funds which are necessary to compete with all the other major record companies.

It's also advisable to have a headquarters say based in America or the UK with representation all over the globe covering all the continents. For example – Empire Music Group (Australia), Empire Music Group (Canada), Empire Music Group (France), Empire Music Group (Brazil), Empire Music Group (South Africa) and Empire Music Group (Japan) etc. You will also need to own subsidiary companies which specialize in different genres of music. For instance – Heavy Metal, Rock, Indie, Country, R&B, Folk, Soul, Pop, Dance and Rap. You could release all the different genres of music on sub-labels, each with different names and which all fall under the umbrella (mother) company which your business is called.

To build your own successful music business requires all the constituent parts that make up the infrastructure of an empire. By doing everything "in—house" as such, you save a lot of money (especially when it comes to marketing the business) in the long term and you will save a lot of time and avoid serious potential problems such as piracy, dirty tricks and delays which can have a major impact on the running of your business. You also stand to generate more income if you do it this way by providing services to third parties. You will also need to be able to provide all the various services to artists and bands signed to your major record company and to also set up all the other types of businesses required to run an effective major record label and run everything smoothly.

Below is a list of all of the sectors within the music industry which you will need to cover and have at your disposal to be able to do everything in-house and in order for your music empire to run smoothly and to be completely independent:

- **Concert Services**

- **Venues**

- **Equipment**

- **Recording Services**

- **Studios**

- **Artists**

- **Business Services**

- **Media**

The following lists describe the personnel (human resources) and types of businesses which are required and which services are essential and desirable to create your own music empire. They also illustrate how much detail goes into each sector of the music business and it gives you some idea of the scale of the operation and the numbers of personnel involved and the businesses required to make things happen. Not just on a national scale, but also on an international scale and global spectrum:

CONCERT SERVICES

- Booking Agents

- Ticket Agents

- Concert Promoters

- Concert Hire

- Festival & Outdoor Event Services

- Catering

- Live Sound & Video Recording Services

- Merchandising

- PA Hire

- Live Sound Engineers

- Production Rehearsal Facilities

- Rigging

- Security

- Tour Production/Tour Managers

- Tour Supplies

- Transport – Air Charter

- Transport – Air & Sea Freight

- Transport – Chauffeur Drive/Limousines

- Transport – Coaches

- Transport – Courier Services

- Transport – Ramps

- Transport – Splitters/Self-Drive

- Transport – Trucking

- Travel Agents

- International Tour Support

VENUES

- Clubs

- Arenas

- Festival Sites

- Concert Halls

The easiest way to guarantee that artist's and bands signed to your record company are able to put on gigs, national and international tours is by owning or renting the venues. You may find it difficult to put gigs and tours on if you don't. If you already have the infrastructure in place, it will enable you to promote and release music in a coordinated fashion and then put on a tour easily without any hitches or hiccups along the way.

EQUIPMENT

- Studio Equipment Hire
- Studio Equipment Manufacture & Distribution

RECORDING SERVICES

- Recording Studios
- Mobile Studios
- Producers
- Producer Management
- Sound Engineers
- Mixers
- Songwriters
- Rehearsal Studios
- Session Fixers
- Studio Design & Construction

Major record companies will often own the recording studio's they use to record artists and bands which are signed to their roster. This helps to reduce any overheads and keeps costs down to a minimum from a business perspective and increases the chances of making a profit and a return on the investment which a record company has shelved out in order to manufacture and release an artist or band's music.

STUDIOS

- Recording Studios
- Mastering Studios

ARTISTS

- Solo Artists

- Bands

- DJ's

- Session Musicians

BUSINESS SERVICES

- Retailers

- Retail Services

- Direct Order Companies

- Record Companies

- Video & DVD Companies

- Music Publishing Companies

- Music Portals

- Download & Mail Order Websites

- Physical Distribution Services

- Mobile Delivery & Distribution Services

- Web Design

- Streaming Websites

- Online Magazines

- Online Delivery & Distribution Services

- Pressers & Duplicators

- Mastering & Post Production

- Printers & Packaging

- Art & Creative Studios

- Merchandise Companies

- Physical Distribution Services

- Industry Organisations

- Accountants

- Legal Services

- Insurance Services

- Financial Advisors

- Artist Management

- Recruitment Services

- Conferences, Exhibitions & Events

- Business Consultants

- Education Services

- Awards Ceremonies

By creating your own award ceremonies you can reward artists and bands signed to your record company and give them recognition for their achievements and also gain major exposure for their music on TV and in magazines at the same time through the coverage gained from these events which also helps gain more publicity and sell more copies of records.

MEDIA

- Newspapers

- Magazines

- Radio Stations – Online & FM

- Television – Music Channels

- Production Music Services

- Broadcast Services

- Advertising Agencies

- Video Production Services

- Promoters & Pluggers

- PR Companies

- Photographers & Agencies

You will need to own your own newspapers and magazines for reviews, articles, adverts and free promo giveaways such as CD's on the front cover of the magazines or newspapers which feature the artists and bands signed to your major record company. This will help reduce costs. It will also help to own your own group of radio station's to achieve maximum airplay both nationally and internationally and also your own music channel's on TV like MTV to get exposure on those mediums. You can also create your own music charts and feature your artists and bands which are signed to your major record company.

If you cover the press side of the music business by having your own media representation such as physical music magazines and online music magazines, it will enable you to advertise music releases when a single or album is scheduled for release and you will be able to include features on artists and bands signed to your record label and you will also be able to include reviews of their music. I would also advise you to work together as a team with like-minded people all under the same umbrella group or company if you do not own any media companies. It will help your business if you can gain maximum publicity for acts signed to your roster through the media. This is how you build your own music empire!

So, if you want to set about creating your own music business, you will need to cover every single aspect of the music industry. It is necessary that you cover all areas of the retail side of the business by opening your own chain of record stores, both online and offline. In other words bricks and mortar record shops or stores and online music retailers. It is also a necessity to have your own music venues where artists and bands can perform live. You will also need your own radio stations, again, both online and offline radio stations. And you will be required to have your own music channels on TV. If you can cover all these sides of the music business, then you are well on your own way to creating your own music empire and the music which you release and the tours which you organize are more likely to be a smash hit and pay dividends.

As you can see from the extensive list above, there are many elements which go into signing an artist or band, making a record, marketing them, releasing their music and putting on gigs etc. A lot of the time you can outsource and sub-contract the work out to reputable and reliable firms but the main thing here is about doing everything in-house and keeping costs down to a minimum by owning all the separate departments required to make a successful record company.

Not only are you creating jobs and mass employment for hundreds of thousands or millions of people in the world, you will also generate different types of income from all the different businesses you own. By implementing all of these strategies and having all these crucial elements in place which I have demonstrated to you in this final chapter of my book, you give all the artists and bands on your roster a much more increased chance of succeeding in the music industry and most importantly the whole infrastructure of your music empire creates long term employment for people and sustainability.

There will be less chance of your business failing and ending up bankrupt! I cannot begin to stress how important this is. If you want to compete for market share of the music business with the likes of Sony BMG, Warner Music Group and the Universal Music Group etc., it's imperative that you follow all of the steps and guidelines outlined in this book! Some record labels prefer to be independents. That's fair enough. I can understand why some people choose to do this and remain independent, but by becoming a major player in the music industry, you've more chance of thriving and being a very profitable business if you create an empire. Most independent record label's go out of business within the first 10-20 years on average whereas major record companies can outlive the independents and merge together with other existing major record companies to secure their market share and save jobs and livelihoods.

Most major record companies have been going in some shape or form for a very long time. They know all the ins and outs of the music business. They have a vast amount of experience. They've lived and they've learnt from mistakes in the past! They use tried and tested methods which work very well and have a proven track record and have proven to be hugely successful over the last century. The current big four major record companies in the world have learnt from experience and practice makes perfect as they say. They have the infrastructure in place to make things happen quickly and to overcome any obstacles that may come up such as new advances in technology or shifting trends or competition from other record labels. A major record company also has access to a legal team to deal with legal issues and to abide with different laws in different countries and states and also an accountant to keep all the accounts in order.

You will also require great leadership and organizational skills in order to run a major record company. It will help if you have previous experience working in the music industry or running a large corporation. It is not something you can just jump feet first into without any prior experience and do on your own either. You will need to share the workload and delegate all the different roles to all of your staff. It takes a team effort and involves a lot of work and a large number of people to make a very profitable record company. You will also need diplomacy and good listening skills. As with most empires, nothing lasts forever, so you will always have to stay one step ahead of the game and be adapting to threats and to be aware of your weaknesses whilst recognizing your strengths and taking any opportunities which come along.

Well, that just about concludes all the chapters in this book. I hope you have thoroughly enjoyed reading it and it has given you the tools you need to succeed in the music industry. Whether you're an established musician, a novice, just starting out in a band or as a solo artist, or if you are a DJ, a manager, or if you are a budding music business entrepreneur or music mogul, or just someone reading this book out of pure curiousity, I hope you have found this book very interesting to read and if you're looking at starting your own music business, then I wish you the very best of luck and success with your new venture. I hope you have found my book to be very informative and helpful. All the best in your future endeavours!

AFTERWORD

There are a few things which I didn't mention about in any of the chapters of this book. Not because I left anything out intentionally, it's just because I've only just remembered some things and some new information has come up. So, I am taking this opportunity to discuss a few other matters about my experiences in the music industry and issues which I feel are very relevant to the theme of this book and which you, dear reader would benefit from knowing.

The PRS For Music

It recently came to light whilst I was writing this book, that the PRS For Music which is a royalty collecting society as I've explained before, and they are an organization which is supposed to represent songwriters. They are taking a 65/35 split in their favour for royalties generated from streams on services such as Spotify. This is pure greed in my opinion and a total disregard for artists such as myself. It shows a complete lack of respect towards artists when they are supposed to represent songwriters. Things are bad enough as it is with never receiving royalties for music which is on streaming services such as Spotify and having never received any royalties from sales of my records on other record labels in the past. I was never consulted about this deal and they are not very transparent when it comes to issues like these. I never agreed to this split either. I am in complete shock with regards to this new discovery. Things just seem to be getting worse and worse.

I find it completely outrageous that an organization which is held in such high regard and esteem and which is supposed to represent songwriters can do this. The PRS For Music are making a lot of money from representing songwriters without ever having paid them for the right to exploit their music in this way. If I was signed to a music publishing company, they would pay me an advance fee to exploit my back catalogue of music and license it to third parties. It actually makes their (PRS For Music) behaviour worse than some of the record labels which I was signed to and dealt with in the past. At least, the record labels agreed to deals and consulted me on them whereas the PRS For Music have never even bothered to do this.

This is totally unacceptable and highly unprofessional and now puts this organization in another light. I am currently in the process of investigating how much the PRS For Music made from past releases of mine which I registered with them in the early noughties. Looking back, I was unaware of what split they were taking from those records and what the deal was when I registered my repertoire of music with them. I very much doubt I'll ever do business with them again. From now on, I will license my own music to third parties or sign a music publishing deal with reputable companies (if there is any such thing these days?).

I also recently realized that Chris Steriopulos (DJ Chris Sterio), the so called friend which helped launch my Progressive House/Trance career on his record label – Source Of Gravity Records based in the Isle Of Man (which is a tax haven by the way!) and who I met during my time at University had fraudulently claimed songwriting credits on all of my Source Of Gravity, Outlanders and 4th Orbit tracks and had received royalties for these records as a songwriter. I have tried to contact him about this serious matter and he has refused to talk to me and just ignores any correspondence I have with him. I will continue to persevere with this matter. Even if it means taking legal action at some point in the future.

I have since tried calling Chris on the phone number which I presumed was his. The number is no longer recognized. He has closed down his old website too. He also (technically) currently owes me thousands in unpaid licensing fees for music which was re-released and made available to download and stream. I have tried contacting him on Facebook and he still ignores me. It's like he has something to hide and his behaviour towards me suggests I've been scammed by him and his colleagues in the past. As a result of all of this, I have come to the conclusion that it is a waste of time making electronic dance music for other people and signing to small record labels. They are not interested in the artists and promoting and marketing them and supporting their careers. They are only interested in themselves and promoting their own record labels (brands) and in-house DJ's.

It is my recommendation, that you are better off releasing your own music on your own label and promoting it yourself. These small record labels don't invest any money in you at all and are only interested in making money for themselves and obtaining DJ gigs to supplement their own income. Apart from providing a platform to release your music on, they serve very little purpose other than that. You are just providing them with free products to release and sell at your expense. They are not prepared to invest in artists and develop their careers. In my case, very few people have ever heard of me or my music despite having over 35 releases in the early noughties. The only people that know of my music were the DJ's at the time. It was a complete waste of my time.

No wonder I ended up bankrupt and in financial difficulty! It might seem like nothing and very trivial to some people, but every penny counts when you're making music. The only analogy I can give you is that whereas music is concerned, it is like a pizza. Everyone else takes all the slices of pizza and the musicians are left with none. So, the musicians go hungry and can't pay their bills and get treated like crap in most cases. This kind of behaviour needs to stop and change. Slavery needs to be abolished and it needs to be made a criminal offence to exploit musicians in this way. There are many organisations adopting anti-slavery policies now which is helpful but it doesn't go far enough unfortunately. This is partly why I wrote this book to help raise awareness and lead the way and expose a lot of these people and bring about real change and also educate the younger generations, so that they don't have to go through what some of us have been through and endure such bad treatment.

Chris falsely claimed songwriting royalties from the MCPS (as it was known then) which stands for the Mechanical Copyright Protection Society between April 2004 and December 2008. This organization later merged with the PRS and became known as the PRS For Music. It is quite possible that he earned more royalties that I am unaware of at this present time. Chris made a dishonest living from music in the short time that I was involved with him and his brother – Oliver Steriopulos, as part of the Source Of Gravity production team. That is very apparent. I am in no doubt about that whatsoever. I believe Chris still does the same thing with other artists and takes a lot of credit from music releases. Whether he uses them as ghost producers, I have no idea!

Chris was only involved in the songwriting of one track which we did together called: Source Of Gravity "Perseverance". I wrote the music and performed the vocals on this particular track whereas he wrote the lyrics. This is the only song which Chris had any input on with regards to songwriting. Other tracks which Chris and his brother Olly had input on were only in the form of providing spoken vocal samples. These other songs did not constitute songwriting credits. Even production credits were questionable. Both him and Olly claimed songwriting credits on tracks which they had no input on whatsoever! Neither of them can play a musical instrument. Neither of them are vocalists. Neither of them have any qualifications in music or understand music theory. This is the trouble with a lot of DJ's in the electronic dance music scene. They think they are musicians and can make music. They are completely delusional in my opinion!

On every Source Of Gravity and Outlanders releases on 12" vinyl on Chris's record labels, it clearly states: "Written and Produced by Mark Wheawill and Chris Steriopulos". This simply was not true. The majority of the time, Chris and Olly Steriopulos were mere spectators whilst I was working on tracks in my bedroom studio when I lived at home with my parents. They claimed production and songwriting credits on pretty much every track that I did that was released on their record labels – Source Of Gravity Records and Gravitation Records. How come this type of behaviour is not classed as criminality? It seems as where the electronic dance music business is concerned, anything goes!

Chris Steriopulos built his business (Source Of Gravity Records and Gravitation Records) and DJ'ing career off the back of my name and music! It was me that invested most of my money in buying all the studio equipment for my studio to produce the tracks and get up to the level that was required to get music played by the superstar DJ's at the time and I took a huge financial risk in those days by doing it mostly on credit. Chris DJ'd all over the globe as a result of my music and artists sent in their demo's and signed to his label as a result of the success with my tracks. It was me who really built the foundations for his record labels and brought him success. This is what happens when you get involved with total strangers. It's advisable to get to know people really well before you ever get involved with them in business otherwise the chances are you will be screwed over in some way. The dance music scene really is a law unto themselves! That is my first-hand experience of the scene.

Chris is an absolute charlatan. He told me that he makes electronic dance music as a hobby these days in recent communications with him before he started to ignore me. But yet, he has a music publishing deal with 23rd Precinct which is based in Glasgow, Scotland. I found this out through research I did on the PRS For Music's members website. As soon as you start selling your music on ITunes and Spotify etc. for commercial gain, it is no longer considered as a hobby.

The guy is a pathological liar. I am now in the process of considering legal action against him for the royalties which he claimed in the past which he was not entitled to. If anything, it will be for a moral victory. There is no room in the music business for deception and dishonesty.

People within the music industry, especially the dance music scene, act and operate like a criminal organization. Very much like the mafia. They are very controlling and can be complete and utter control freaks when they want to be. They can also be very negative about some artists especially if there is a vested interest in the money side of the business. Also, Chris used to slag off his Uncle to me when I knew him in my university days and when I was releasing music on his record labels. He was very negative about his uncle and musicians in general and I got the general impression that deep down he was very jealous and envious of musicians and wanted to be a musician and superstar DJ himself, but was too lazy to learn and put the time and effort in. His Uncle, Philip Steriopulos was a musician in the famous band – Fairground Attraction, and also had mental health problems according to Chris. Eddie Reader was the singer and they had a hit single with "Perfect" in the year 1988.

Spotify and Streaming Services

If streaming is to become a viable format, then I would suggest that services like Spotify introduce a subscription per release business model and system. Music consumers would have to subscribe to each artist's album and single releases as opposed to simply subscribing to streaming services such as Spotify to listen to as much music as they would like. It makes no business sense whatsoever for artists at this current moment in time as there is very little revenue to share amongst digital music content providers. Spotify, for example, only generate income from subscribing to their service and also from advertising revenue. The music industry cannot survive on this current business model and it is not sustainable. The industry will eventually collapse and this is why I will not include my own music releases on such services.

Artists are being conned by Spotify and other streaming services and they are laughing all the way to the bank. Music consumers should be subscribing to each release as opposed to subscribing to the service – Spotify as a whole. As I have stated before, most people in the music industry don't have a clue what they're doing. At this current time, it's all trial and error. It proves my suspicion when artists get over excited at the number of total combined plays (streams) on streaming services. Artists and record labels are being scammed by services such as Spotify. They are also being played by the consumers as in they are being had over.

The statistics for millions of streams mean nothing to me. When one million people subscribe to each music release and Spotify start paying royalties based on a subscription per release business model, then that is something to get really excited about. Spotify are screwing the artists over at the moment and so are the fans. Artists literally are being "played" by both parties when it comes to Spotify and streaming services in general. For the time being, until things change, you are better off sticking to releasing your music on physical formats. When a subscription per release business model is introduced, I may change my mind about streaming as a viable format.

The difference with me is that I am not a fool unlike the majority of other artists and people working in the music industry. I have been stung before and majorly screwed over and as you know, I ended up bankrupt. So, I have learnt my lesson from this and I have become a much better businessman in the process and as a result. I have spent years on the sidelines and have been monitoring the situation very closely. Artists who release their music on Spotify using the current business model come across as if they're desperate for their music to be heard. I call this desperation music marketing. It is sheer desperation on their part. It has taken me a very long time to bounce back. I will not make the same mistakes again. So, I hope you will take my advice and tread carefully when it comes to streaming as a format to release your music on to the public. Please don't make the mistakes that everyone else is making. It will just end up in tears.

Commercial Radio

I also would like to add a point about commercial radio. It is very expensive to get your music onto their radio stations and they still take bribes and backhanders to get your music onto playlists. Radio play is not necessarily based on the merits of the music. It is a lot easier for independent record labels and artists to get their music aired and played on non-commercial radio stations or college radio stations and internet radio. You are more likely to get heard and included on playlists if you send your music to smaller radio stations. Competition for airplay is very fierce on commercial radio stations and it can cost you thousands to get featured on playlists. This basically rules commercial radio out as an option for new and unsigned artists. The music industry is very hard to break into. I am in no doubt about that and you need to be very aware of this before embarking on a music career as an independent artist or record label.

Vitality

There's another issue I have with people who have used my artist name - "Vitality" on their own music releases since I ended up ill in 2005. I suspect other people were cashing in on my name and my success with my first Vitality single "Skylite" and my debut album which was released on my own label: TSYT Recordings in 2004 and they were capitalizing on this whilst I was ill and absent from the music business during the period 2005 – 2017. I know of at least 5 other artists and DJ's from all over the world who have been using my artist name "Vitality". I have contacted as many of them as possible to stop using that name and threatened them with legal action as I released music as far back as 2003 on Method Records under the Vitality artist name.

An artist using my Vitality name released a trance track a few years ago. I suspect that labels I was signed to i.e. Method Records and Baroque Records based in Coventry, UK, may have been behind this. Who knows? The electronic dance music scene is a law unto themselves and I'm not sure I ever want to be a part of it ever again. It's nothing but trouble and it's a cut-throat business, make no mistake about that! These people must be so desperate for money and are too lazy to build up their own name, that they will go to all kinds of extremes just to make money from music. It's a very weird game that they play. It's all extremely disturbing and there is no love in the dance music scene. It's all false and most of the people involved in it are fake. I am certain other well-known artists in that music scene have experienced similar problems. It would be interesting to hear what they have to say on such matters.

I also noticed lots of corporations also starting to use the name "Vitality" on other products after I released my first album in the last decade or so. For example, breakfast cereals in supermarkets and insurance companies in the UK. I sent off numerous copies of my first album – Vitality "Vitality" on CD which was released on my first label TSYT RECORDINGS in 2004, in about the period between 2005-2006 to many corporations during the time I was suffering from real financial troubles and just before I became really ill with mental health problems. I wrote to them looking for sponsorship deals to try and get out of the debt I was in at the time as well as merger proposals with music companies such as EMI Music. I was very desperate for help at the time, so it made perfect sense to approach other organisations. What harm could it do? At the same time, I needed help but was also in a position to assist them especially with the crisis the music industry was experiencing at the time with piracy and digital downloads.

It does not bother me that lots of corporations started to use the name "Vitality" on various products as it's a generic word in the dictionary. But the issue with other artists around the globe using my name on their music releases was a real problem. I was not in a position to take legal action against them. However, I did approach download stores and streaming services to initiate a takedown process. But, in the end I gave up and thought it was not worth the hassle. I decided to continue to use my Vitality artist name on some music projects and start using my own name more on future releases. Using pseudonyms is counter-productive too be honest. If they have a problem with me using the Vitality name on music productions, then let them come to me. I came up with that artist name first in 2003 and I have the proof. They won't stand a chance in a court of law if it comes down to it. But I do take real issue with people using my Vitality artist name to cash in on it.

Corruption

This is the type of corruption that a lot of us artists have to deal with in the music industry. Not to mention that a career in the music business can also be a matter of life and death. There are many stars who've died young! For example: Karen Carpenter (The Carpenters), Michael Jackson (Jackson Five), Kurt Cobain (Nirvana), Amy Winehouse and Freddie Mercury (Queen). The list is endless. Getting involved in the music industry and becoming famous appears to end up taking people's lives. Is it a price worth paying I ask? That's the million dollar question! I don't think it's worth it. It would seem there is a dark side to the music business. The more I look into it all and investigate, the darker it seems. The devil really is leading people astray in this world. The music industry nearly destroyed me and took my soul. I will admit that. But I am a born survivor. I am a fighter and I don't quit easily. I am a lot more stronger than people realize.

In a nutshell, the music industry is just as corrupt as any other industry in the world and it can end up killing you if you're not careful! So, please do take care and look after yourself, dear reader. I hope reading this book has provided you with a great insight into the music industry and that you will be able to market and sell your music and survive the music business in the

21st century. I wish you every bit of success with your endeavours. I hope other artists speak out in the future about the music business and help educate the next generations, so that they don't have to go through what we've been through. For me, in the early days, it was a constant struggle. Hopefully, this is the start of a new era! If you ever need any music industry advice you know where to find me.

Mark Wheawill - September 2018

APPENDIX

DISCOGRAPHY

Mark Wheawill

12" VINYL

- Source Of Gravity "Full Moon/Winter's Discontent" (White Label) (Source Of Gravity Recore 2000

- Source Of Gravity "Futuristic Visions" (Source Of Gravity Records) 2000

- Source Of Gravity "Deception" (Source Of Gravity Records) 2001

- Source Of Gravity "Full Moon" (Source Of Gravity Records) 2001

- Mark Wheawill "Angell's Kiss" (Source Of Gravity Records) 2001

- Source Of Gravity "Lindside" (Dorigen Music) 2001

- Source Of Gravity "Metallic Groove" (Gravitation) 2001

- Outlanders "Silent Conflict" (Gravitation) 2001

- Mark Wheawill "Tension" (Gravitation) 2001

- Source Of Gravity "Atlantis" (Source Of Gravity Records) 2001

- Source Of Gravity "Fusion"/"Cydonia" (Mechanism) 2001

- Outlanders "Ice" (Source Of Gravity Records) 2001

- Source Of Gravity "Overload"/"Sacrifice" (Three) 2002

- TSYT "Colorblind" (Source Of Gravity Records) 2002

- 4th Orbit "Deep Isolation" (Gravitation) 2002

- Mark Wheawill "Darkside" (Source Of Gravity Records) 2002

- Bravemusic "Spiritualized" (Method Records) 2002

- Evenflow "Indecisive" (Baroque Records) 2002

- Vitality "Skylite" (Method Records) 2002

- Mark Wheawill "Transition" (Baroque Records) 2003

- Source Of Gravity "Perseverance" (Pied Piper Records) 2003

- Source Of Gravity "Resonance" (Source Of Gravity Records) 2003

- Sterio & Wheawill "Spellbound" (Source Of Gravity Records) 2003

- Vitality "Chemistry/Blinded By The Sun(Ode To BT)" (TSYT Recordings) 2005

- Mark Wheawill "Written In The Stars" (Uplifted Music) 2018

- Vitality "Don't Panic" (Uplifted Music) 2018

- Vitality "Party's Just Started/Golden Virginia" (Uplifted Music) 2018

- Vitality "Addicted To Love/Chemistry (Radio Edit)/Scratch" (Uplifted Music) 2018

119

- Vitality "Love Story/Letting Go" (Uplifted Music) 2018

- Mark Wheawill "Love Will Save The Day" (Uplifted Music) 2018

- Mark Wheawill "May The Force Be With You" (Uplifted Music) 2018

- Mark Wheawill "Light Years Ahead" (Uplifted Music) 2018

MP3's

- Vitality "Mental Block" (TSYT Recordings Ltd) 2006

- Mark Wheawill "Written In The Stars" (Uplifted Music) 2019

- Mark Wheawill "Love Will Save The Day" (Uplifted Music) 2019

- Mark Wheawill "May The Force Be With You" (Uplifted Music) 2019

- Mark Wheawill "Light Years Ahead" (Uplifted Music) 2019

- Mark Wheawill "Love Rules The Day" (Uplifted Music) 2019

- Mark Wheawill "I Need You Tonight" (Uplifted Music) 2019

- Mark Wheawill "Lovestruck Opus 1, No. 1" (Uplifted Music) 2019

WAV

- Mark Wheawill "Written In The Stars" (Uplifted Music) 2018

- Mark Wheawill "Love Will Save The Day" (Uplifted Music) 2018

- Mark Wheawill "May The Force Be With You" (Uplifted Music) 2018

- Mark Wheawill "Light Years Ahead" (Uplifted Music) 2018

SINGLE RELEASES – REMIXES

12" VINYL

- Trey Smith "Collection" Outlanders Remix (Gravitation) 2002

- Alexander Church "Welcome to my world" Mark Wheawill Remix (Gravitation) 2002

- Mezo "Superconscious" Mark Wheawill Remix (Source Of Gravity Records) 2002

- Rowan Blades & Naughty G "Webcore" Tilt Remix (Rocksteady Records) 2003

ALBUM RELEASES

CD's

- Vitality "Vitality" (TSYT Recordings) 2004

MP3

- Vitality "Vitality" (Uplifted Music) 2010 (Re-release)

STREAMING

- Vitality "Vitality" (Uplifted Music) 2010 (Re-release)

WAV

- Vitality "Vitality" (Uplifted Music) 2018 (Special Re-release)

- Vitality "The White Album" (Uplifted Music) 2018 (Bonus Album)

- Vitality "The Black Album" (Uplifted Music) 2018 (Bonus Album)

COMPILATIONS

CD's:

- Spacer - Europes Future Anthems - Source Of Gravity "Futuristic Visions" (Planetworks Ltd) 2000

- Singularity 02 - Source Of Gravity "Deception" (United Recordings) 2001

- Baroque in Session 2002 - Evenflow "Indecisive" & Bravemusic "Spiritualized" 2002

La Rocca - Marko on Sundays/2002 Vol. 1 - Alexander Church "Welcome to my world" [Mark Wheawill Remix] (541) 2002

PW01 - Evenflow "Indecisive" (Trust the DJ) 2002

Solid Sounds Anno 2003 Vol 1 - Vitality "Skylite" (541/pias) 2003

Coors Light Party AGoGo - Mark Wheawill "Transition" [Future House Remix] (High Note Records) 2004

Daniel Bruns & Taucher present Eye-Trance 10 - Alexander Church "Welcome to my world" [Mark Wheawill Remix] (Cue Point Records) 2005

STREAMING

Uplifted Music: Cancer Research UK Dance Music Compilation (Uplifted Music) 2010

USEFUL LINKS

Websites

UPLIFTED MUSIC & MEDIA PORTAL

www.upliftedmusic.co.uk

UPLIFTED MARKETING

www.upliftedmarketing.co.uk

MIXCLOUD – DJ MIXES

www.mixcloud.com/markwheawill

SOUNDCLOUD – AUDIO CLIPS & DJ MIXES

www.soundcloud.com/markwheawill

www.soundcloud.com/uplifted-music-uk

Social Media

FACEBOOK

Facebook.com/musicindustryadvice

Facebook.com/upliftedmarketing

Facebook.com/upliftedmusicmediaportal

INSTAGRAM

Instagram.com/markwheawillofficial

TWITTER

Twitter.com/upliftedmusicuk

Do you want to know how to market and sell your music in the 21st century? Do you want to know how to get funding for your music projects and to be able to record, manufacture, distribute and release your own music or an artist or a which you represent? Are you looking for insider tips and advice music industry? Do you want to know how to build your own music empir

This book is the answer to all of your prayers and it answers all and more. It contains the blueprints for a Music label of the 21st century. It is a modern day cians, complete beginners, established preneurs. It gives you a deep espec

How To Market And Sell Your Music And the Music Busi Century is part biography a industry advice. It covers related to the music busines Eye-opener and This is the first major work author - Mark Whe his field. He is one of the respected artists in the electronic music scene who deser recognition for his contribution to electronic dance music the early noughties. His book also demonstrate his vision for the this forward thinking and revolutionary approaches and selling music, this century.

the most comprehensive guides to the music business that been written and it also gives you an insight into the early stages of the Mark Wheewill's music career and how to survive the music business in century. It is a book which you will treasure for the rest of your life and inform and enlighten you about the secrets of the music business like no her

Printed by Amazon Italia Logistica S.r.l.
Torrazza Piemonte (TO), Italy